My

Conversations

With Angels

About the Author

Judith Marshall has a BA in History, an MA in Linguistics, and a lifelong passion for the paranormal. Childhood encounters with the spirit world sparked more than twenty-five years of research and travel which connected her with countless others—from newbies to professional psychics—who divulged similar experiences. Inspired by their stories, further study, continuing personal experience, and psychic insights from her own children, she resolved to use the written word to raise awareness of and respect for spiritual metaphysics.

To Write to the Author

If you wish to contact the author or would like more information about this book, please write to the author in care of Llewellyn Worldwide, and we will forward your request. Both the author and publisher appreciate hearing from you and learning of your enjoyment of this book and how it has helped you. Llewellyn Worldwide cannot guarantee that every letter written to the author can be answered, but all will be forwarded. Please write to:

Judith Marshall
c/o Llewellyn Worldwide
2143 Wooddale Drive
Woodbury, MN 55125-2989

Please enclose a self-addressed stamped envelope for reply; or $1.00 to cover costs. If outside the USA, enclose an international postal reply coupon.

$\mathscr{M}$Y

$\mathscr{C}$ONVERSATIONS

$\mathscr{W}$ITH $\mathscr{A}$NGELS

Inspirational Moments with Guardian Spirits

Judith Marshall

Llewellyn Worldwide
Woodbury, Minnesota

FIRST EDITION
First Printing, 2012

Editing by Laura Graves
Book design by Bob Gaul
Cover design by Ellen Lawson
Cover art: Background © iStockphoto.com./Kim Sohee
        White feather © iStockphoto.com/Brian Jackson
        Sunny grass © iStockphoto.com/cunfek

Llewellyn Publications is a registered trademark of Llewellyn Worldwide Ltd.

Library of Congress Cataloging-in-Publication Data
Marshall, Judith, 1968–
  My conversations with angels: inspirational moments with guardian spirits/
Judith Marshall.—1st ed.
      p. cm.
  Includes bibliographical references
  ISBN 978-0-7387-3286-2
1. Spirits—Miscellanea. 2. Angels—Miscellanea. I. Title.
  BF1999.M275 2012
  202´.15—dc23
                              2012023810

Llewellyn Publications
A Division of Llewellyn Worldwide Ltd.
2143 Wooddale Drive
Woodbury, MN 55125-2989
www.llewellyn.com

Printed in the United States of America

ℭONTENTS

$\mathcal{I}$ NTRODUCTION

$\mathbf{A}$ngels are all around us. Their population greatly exceeds our own, and you have at least one with you right this moment—no exceptions. In fact, it's very likely that an angel guided you to this book, so you could learn more about the plethora of spiritual beings among us and allow them to work with you on a regular basis.

I'm not just whistling Dixie; I know from personal experience that angels, guardians, and guides—in whatever guise they present themselves—are real. Although I'm not a professional psychic or medium, I have received confirmations from professionals and other psychically attuned individuals more times than I can count. I'm just an average person, but my open mind and heart have paved the way for angelic communication. Everyone is capable of the same.

When I was sixteen, I experienced something incredible, but the circumstances surrounding it were as commonplace as could be. One of my teachers had given me permission to leave her classroom, so I crossed a deserted hallway and headed upstairs. Near the top of the stairs, my foot missed a step and I started to fall backwards.

A sudden force on my back shoved me into a vertical position. I gasped, and once I regained my step, turned to see who'd saved me.

I was alone on the stairway.

A decade later, I was rushing home from work, and the sidewalk was slick with melting snow. The cumbersome bags in my hands consumed my attention, so I failed to spot a patch of ice. My heel slid and I started to fall backwards. Across the street, a fellow pedestrian screamed. She and I both knew the angle between my back and the pavement spelled disaster.

In a flash, I was lifted and righted in mid-air, then placed back onto the sidewalk. I froze, stunned by the miracle. Then I locked eyes with the woman across the street. She was gaping at me, for she'd had a better view of what happened. I'd only felt it.

I gave her an awkward smile. She sighed and lowered the hand she'd flung to her chest.

"Thank God!" she exclaimed.

My thoughts exactly.

I believe angels saved me in both instances.

Years later, my husband and I welcomed identical twin boys into our family. They displayed psychic awareness from the get-go and often spoke of angels and other spirits they spotted around the house, in the yard, in the car, at amusement parks, and even at the grocery store.

Like most children, they had more than one dance with danger. Parents know what I'm talking about: those horrific, heart-stopping moments when—despite your best efforts—your children tumble down stairs, slam their heads against the pavement, or sink to the bottom of a pool during their first, supposedly supervised swimming lesson. After a number of these experiences, my children described the "flying" beings of light who instantly appeared to save them.

Onlookers and an emergency room doctor dubbed one such episode a miracle. Just before it occurred, a premonition of danger seized me, and I asked angels to surround my boys with a cushion of love that would protect them. After the drama, I had one burning question: did the angels intervene because I called them or were they just manning their posts?

Maybe you've had similar questions, sparked by natural curiosity or key moments that made you do a double take: a gut instinct proven correct, a strange calm that enfolded you during a crisis, one "coincidence" too many, or a suspicion that you weren't alone, even though you were the only one in the room! Such encounters make us contemplate the nature of the spirit world and how it works.

Guidance, protection, and inspiration are literal godsends, and who among us would refuse them? Life is tough enough without ignoring the divine network that shimmers within and around us. Socrates, Jesus, Muhammad, George Frideric Handel, George Washington, William Blake, Ralph Waldo Emerson, Nikola Tesla, Ernest Shackleton, Carl Jung, J. R. R. Tolkien, and Charles Lindbergh had some of the better known experiences, but "supernatural" support exists for all of us.

Opinions differ—based on cultural or religious beliefs, research, intuition, and/or personal experience—but no one holds a monopoly on the truth. There's always more to learn, and we should be curious! As the French philosopher Pierre Teilhard de Chardin once said, "We are not human beings having a spiritual experience. We are spiritual beings having a human experience."

The least we can do is look into the matter. The best we can do is keep an open mind, erase some of the question marks, and develop a working relationship with those benevolent beings known as angels, guardians, and guides.

1

Angels: History and Hierarchy

Angels are the loving thoughts of God made manifest. If the title "God" makes you uncomfortable, please substitute any term that feels right: Universal Intelligence, Great Spirit, God-Goddess, Creator, Supreme Being, All That Is, the Source, Ein Sof, etc. Angels, too, are known by a variety of names, but in essence, they are beings composed of light, love, and intelligence who safeguard the balance of the universe.

Linguistically, the word "angel" comes from the Latin *angelus,* borrowed from the Greek term for "messenger," *angelos.* It's also related to the ancient Persian *angaros* ("mounted courier") and Sanskrit *angíras,* a luminous being who mediated between humans and the world of the gods. The concept of divine messengers—of supernatural intermediaries—touched a great many cultures, but when it comes to angelology, a Persian prophet named Zarathustra, a.k.a. Zoroaster, set the stage.

Although scholars accept him as a real historical figure, they have yet to agree on when he lived. Estimates range between the eighteenth and sixth centuries BCE! Regardless of that titanic timespan, Zarathustra developed a detailed cosmology that directly influenced the Judaic notion of angelic beings, which in turn spawned Christian angelology. As Joseph Campbell observed in *The Hero with a Thousand Faces,* "Persian belief was reorganized by the prophet Zarathustra according to a strict dualism of good and evil principles, light and dark, angels and devils. This crisis profoundly affected not only the Persians, but also the subject Hebrew beliefs, and thereby (centuries later) Christianity." Both the Hebrew and Christian traditions then affected the Islamic perception of angels.

Influential as Zoroastrianism became, it was still a newcomer next to the spiritual traditions of ancient Egypt, not to mention those of the Sumerian culture which flourished in the Middle East around 3000 BCE. And no matter where you turn, winged creatures abound in written and pictorial accounts.

But here's the rub: did the wings represent an actual physical attribute or simply a divine ability? After all,

such beings were said to descend from—and ascend to—
the skies and/or "heaven," i.e., the higher dimensions.

Ancient astronaut theorists suggest they did so in
spaceships. Many believe the angels known as the Watchers—
the *Grigori* mentioned in the books of Daniel, Enoch, and
Jubilees and, in earlier Sumerian tales, the *Igigi,* "those
who watch and see"—weren't angels at all but extraterres-
trials or ultraterrestrials (non-human, interdimensional
beings indigenous to Earth) whose deeds inspired a number of mythologies and misinterpretations in the earliest
religious texts. The research on the subject is intriguing,
and some of the theories have merit.

Even if they're true, there's also a spiritual element
to the universe. Humanity's attempt to interpret that
element has resulted in a number of religions, three
of which spread like wildfire across the globe. Inevita-
bly, the angelology of Judaism, Christianity, and Islam
shaped the perceptions of the masses. Let's consider
the traditions of all three.

Judaism

Ancient Persian mythology viewed griffins—winged
creatures depicted in a variety of forms—as benevolent
guardians of light; in Persian, Babylonian, and Assyrian
art, they were symbols of divinity and wisdom. When
the Jewish people came in contact with these symbols
during the Babylonian Exile, they became fascinated
with them. As Richard Webster notes in *Praying with
Angels,* "The Jews were so enamored of the griffin that

they adopted it and made griffins their first angels. In the Book of Exodus, cherubim were posted in the east of Eden after the expulsion of Adam and Eve to make sure that no one entered."

In Genesis, the angel (Hebrew: *mal'akh*, "messenger") who grappled with Jacob assumed a human form—as did the three angels who visited Abraham in the plains of Mamre—but prophets like Ezekiel and Isaiah pointed out the spiritual nature of angels. By the third century BCE, Judaism regarded angels as spirits who appeared to humans as apparitions. Much later, the twelfth-century Jewish philosopher Maimonides described angels as created beings, "totally disembodied minds...which emanate from God and are the intermediaries between God and all the bodies here in this world."

Judaism's heavenly hosts informed men of God's will, disciplined wrongdoers, and defended the faithful against the forces of evil. On the subject of evil, please note that the word "satan" was never a proper name referring to some archenemy of God; in the earliest texts, the Jewish phrase *ha-satan* simply meant "the adversary." In *Guides, Guardians, and Angels*, D. J. Conway emphasizes this fact and indicates that any opponent—from a crabby neighbor to a rabid rival—could qualify as *ha-satan*.

Elaine Pagels's *The Origin of Satan* expounds occasional references to "the satan" in Hebrew texts like the books of Numbers and Job. The term clearly depicts any one of the many angels God sends to thwart or check human action when necessary. Yet this messenger isn't malicious; he's simply doing his job.

Evil wasn't a personage but a personal matter. The Talmud, a huge record of Jewish law, philosophy, and traditions, explained the duality of man's nature as characterized by two "angels"—*yetzer ha-ra* ("the evil impulse") and *yetzer ha-tov* ("the good impulse")—that entered each person after birth. The positive balanced the negative. Placed smack-dab between the two, man could draw closer to his creator through the power of choice, i.e., free will.

Still, many Jews carried talismans or charms to ward off demons and negative spirits. One such amulet was the *kimiyah* ("angel text"). Rabbinical scribes wrote sacred words, like the names of angels or excerpts from the Torah—the five books of Moses: Genesis, Exodus, Leviticus, Numbers, and Deuteronomy—on parchment which they encased in silver or leather and wore on the body.

Christianity

Not surprisingly, Christianity's view of angels built upon the Judaic foundation. Angels attended God's throne and served as executors of his will, so to speak, for they upheld his laws in the physical world. As divine messengers, they dipped their wings into a number of the New Testament's pivotal moments, including the births of John the Baptist and Jesus the Christ, Jesus's "Agony in the Garden," and his all-important resurrection.

Angelology and demonology experienced resurrections of their own. The former discipline grouped celestial beings into seven ranks, which when added to the Old Testament's seraphim and cherubim, resulted in nine choirs of angels. Archangel Michael, who already enjoyed a starring role in Judaic tradition, became a Christian favorite, although he was sometimes confused with the warrior St. George. (More on Michael and other archangels in chapter 3.)

Of course, Christianity increasingly associated *ha-satan*, "the adversary," with a single, supernatural threat and with the Latin name for the morning star, *Lucifer* ("light-bearer" or "light-bringer"), whose mythical fate—to fall from heaven and be "cast down to earth"—described in Isaiah 14:4–17, belonged to an arrogant king of Babylon, not an angel. Related scripture, Revelation 12:7–8, asserted "there was war in heaven: Michael and his angels fought against the dragon; and the dragon fought and his angels, and prevailed not; neither was their place found any more in heaven." Interestingly, parallels to such a downfall already existed in earlier Assyro-Babylonian mythology.

To Christianity, Lucifer/Satan became a fallen angel literally hell-bent on the destruction of man and all things holy. Belief in this diabolical foe, combined with trust in God's grace, spurred Christians toward the use of protective and devotional symbols. Sacramentals like crucifixes, medals, rosaries, and holy water are still among the most popular.

Islam

The belief in angels (Arabic: *Malā'ikah*) is one of Islam's articles of faith. They're mentioned numerous times in the Qur'an and Hadith—the collective report of the prophet Muhammad's statements and actions and their related traditions—and figure prominently in events Jews and Christians would recognize from their own sacred books: the visitation of Ibrahim (Abraham) at the Oak of Mamre in Hebron; the deliverance of Lut (Lot) from Sodom's destruction; and the annunciation and immaculate conception of Isa (Jesus). The Archangel Jibril (Gabriel), whom Muslims regard as the greatest of all angels, is believed to have visited Muhammad a number of times in different forms to dictate the Qur'an to the prophet.

In the Islamic worldview, there are no fallen angels. *Šayṭān*, also called *Iblīs* and the equivalent of Christianity's Satan, is one of the jinn. The jinn, usually invisible to humans, are said to live on earth in a world parallel to ours. They can be good, evil, or neutral in their dealings with humans or each other. They were the same beings—known as demons in *The Testament of Solomon*—who supposedly built the Temple of Jerusalem under King Solomon's command. While possessed of "supernatural" strength, speed, and abilities like shapeshifting and flight, they eat, drink, marry, and procreate. They also die, although the lifespan of a *jinnī* is considerably longer than that of a human. Among their alleged dwelling places are archaeological treasures like Petra in Jordan and Ubar in southern Oman.

According to the Qur'an, *Allah*—another name for "the (sole) deity, God"—created angels from light and jinn from smokeless fire. Like humans, the jinn were created with free will. The angels, however, were not; they do only God's bidding and never tire of worshiping him.

The differences between the three Abrahamic religions are undeniable, but two fundamental beliefs convey a common denominator: 1. there exists one, all-knowing creator; and 2. that creator made angels as functional extensions of its will. The three religions offer a shared vision of how and why angels function.

Angels are messengers who reveal divine truths. Angels praise and serve their creator by helping humanity understand and nurture its connection to divinity.

It's common ground, to be sure, and a great place to start. Yet we still have a lot of territory to explore. Let's press on with answers to some frequently asked questions.

What Do Angels Look Like?

Whether based on symbolic imagery or eyewitness accounts, descriptions of angels run the gamut. They can be exquisitely beautiful humanoids—winged or not, "solid" or see-through, androgynous, male, or female—and seem to glow with an inner light. They can appear as multicolored sparkles, flashes of white light, or ethereal, swirling mists. In their presence, you may feel physical sensations such as a sudden change in air pressure or a soft, tingling caress. The bottom line is that angels are energy, so they can express themselves through whatever form is necessary.

Need an instant bodyguard when you're in danger? *Done.*

An encouraging word from a stranger who vanishes the moment you turn your back? *No problem.*

A dreamtime encounter with a unicorn whose coat is so white it nearly blinds you? *Sure. Whatever works here!*

Plain and simple, angels can project any mental image which helps us. Often, the image is precisely what we anticipate. Do you expect wings? You just might see them. Yet in *Guides, Guardians, and Angels*, D. J. Conway asserts that angel wings are merely streams of energy that accompany their movements. For some people, however, the realization that they've encountered an angel dawns on them after the fact.

Angels are androgynous by nature, so they can appear as male or female. One example: some experts, like Doreen Virtue, PhD, see the Archangel Gabriel as predominantly feminine; others assume this angel is male. In *Azrael Loves Chocolate; Michael's a Jock*, angel intuitive Chantel Lysette revealed that her first encounter with that archangel was with his/her feminine aspect, which she calls "Gabrielle." Because Lysette was uncomfortable with a female authority figure, Gabriel presented his/her masculine side, "Gabe," thereafter.

Since most languages of the world use gender pronouns, talking or writing about androgynous beings can be tricky, and the neutral alternative "it" seems somewhat rude in reference to angels. For the sake of ease, I'll represent angels as male from this point on.

Do Angels Prefer One Religion to Another?

The following quote, attributed to St. Thomas Aquinas, says it best: "Angels transcend every religion, every philosophy, every creed. In fact, angels have no religion as we know it, as their existence precedes every religious system that has ever existed."

In *The Angel Code*, Chantel Lysette complements this concept perfectly with information her spirit guide, Jake, related about his death. Mere seconds after he'd crossed over, Jake evidently met the archangels Raphael, Michael, Gabriel, and Cassiel. Terrified, he admitted to them that he wasn't a Christian. Gabriel glanced at his fellow angels, then regarded Jake with a shrug and said, "Funny, neither are we."

What Types of Angels Exist? How Are They Categorized?

Philosophers and theologians might not have debated how many angels could dance on the head of a pin, but they went all-out to classify the species. Consequently, there's no shortage of celestial hierarchies, including Islamic, Christian, Zoroastrian, and the various Kabbalistic versions. In an effort to keep it simple, we'll look at one of the better-known lists, created in the fifth century by Pseudo-Dionysius the Areopagite and polished in the thirteenth century by St. Thomas Aquinas. While this list determines the order, the information about each level comes from a potpourri of sources, including sacred texts of the three major Abrahamic religions, the work of Rudolf Steiner—founder of Anthroposophy, a philosophy meant to unify science and spirit—and books by modern authors like Richard Webster, D. J. Conway, Doreen Virtue, and Sylvia Browne.

But first, a word about hierarchies. It's best not to think in terms of a pecking order or military chain of command. Picture instead a large company with different departments, each with a vital role to play. One might be more powerful than another but never more important. To paraphrase Deepak Chopra, the universe in its perfection has no spare parts... and that goes for humans, too!

Upper Triad or Choir

These angels have the highest vibration and are therefore closest to the divine core (God) of energy and information.

1. **Seraphim** (*seraph*, singular)—angels of divine love and light whose primary function is to circle God, locked in perpetual adoration, i.e., song; identified as Rudolf Steiner's Spirits of Love; described as having either six fiery red wings or, according to Sylvia Browne, a pair of

silver-tipped, white wings. Guardians of
the Light, they regulate and record the
celestial movements of the universe and
have little contact with humans.

2. **Cherubim** (*cherub*, singular)—the "near
ones" or "carriers" of divine majesty; "the
ones who intercede"; Steiner's Spirits of
Harmony; originally depicted as formidable,
griffinlike creatures, as far from the roly-poly,
Gerber-baby look-alikes in Renaissance
paintings as you can get. Later, the book of
Ezekiel gave them four faces and four wings,
and nowadays, they're portrayed as men with
two, four, or six blue-colored wings or, per
Sylvia Browne, with gold-tipped, white wings.
According to *Sunan Abu Dawood*, the prophet
Muhammad said, "I have been given permission
to speak about one of the angels of God who
carry the Throne. The distance between his
earlobes and his shoulders is equivalent to a
seven-hundred-year journey." Muslim tradition
also holds that the attendants of God's throne
love "the believers" and implore God (Allah)
to forgive human sins. Their chief duties are to
worship God and maintain heaven's records.

3. **Thrones** (also known as *Ophanim*)—the
"wheels" or "many-eyed ones" who convey
God's truth to all; Steiner's Spirits of Will;

described by Browne as having deep purple wings. The Book of Daniel portrays the throne itself as being "like the fiery flame, and his wheels as burning fire." The Thrones are symbols of God's authority. According to St. Thomas Aquinas, they ponder and administer divine justice.

Middle Triad

These angels transform divine energy into usable form, oversee the universe, and carry out God's will.

4. **Dominions**—wise angels who determine and designate the cosmic tasks necessary to the smooth operation of the universe; Steiner's Spirits of Wisdom; said to look like stunningly beautiful humans, usually clad in green and gold, with two feathery wings which, according to Browne, are green. The sword and scepter are their symbols. They supervise and assign duties to the lower choirs, but they themselves receive orders from the Cherubim or Thrones.

5. **Virtues**—the "shining ones" or "strongholds" who develop strategies for the tasks assigned by the Dominions; Steiner's Spirits of Motion; said to wear gold belts around their waists and described by Browne as having pale blue wings. They uphold natural laws—whether they concern the weather or the movement

of planets and stars—and, on occasion,
allow miracles which go against those laws.

6. **Powers**—the "authorities" who perform the
cosmic tasks delegated by the Dominions and
outlined by the virtues; Steiner's Spirits of
Form. As God's loyal warriors, they combat
the forces of darkness and oversee the
distribution of power in the universe.
In *Archangels and Ascended Masters*, Doreen
Virtue describes them as "bouncers" who
prevent negative entities—in human or
spirit form—from taking over the world.
When necessary, they can intervene to guide
disoriented souls or earthbound spirits, a.k.a.
ghosts, to the Other Side.

Lower Triad

These angels communicate God's light and love to individual planets including, in our case, Earth.

7. **Principalities**—the angels who—in cooperation
with the Powers—organize earthly tasks,
look after nations and cities, and on occasion,
create miracles on a national or personal level;
Steiner's Spirits of Personality; according to
Sylvia Browne, they have golden wings and
intervene only when our explicit call for them
coincides with God's command. They work with
the guardian angels of each person and place.

8. **Archangels**—extremely powerful angels who perform tasks designated by the Principalities and serve as God's chief messengers; Steiner's Spirits of Fire or Folk; described by Browne as having pure white wings. According to Chantel Lysette, wing color varies depending on the archangel. Doreen Virtue also associates different colors with specific archangels. (Details on archangels in chapter 3.)

9. **Angels**—the "carriers of prayers" and "watchers who never sleep"; Steiner's Sons of Life or Twilight; those closest to humans and therefore our immediate channels of divine energy; distinguished from other angels by their gray-white wings. Guardian angels arc included in this group. (More on guardian angels in chapter 6.)

So there you have it: nine levels, three choirs, one source. Remember, that source is unconditional love. Angels don't expect us to be perfect. They don't marinate in judgment or itch to smite humans at the first opportunity.

Sure, their messages might annoy you at times, like when they encourage you to step outside of your comfort zone or gently remind you that the triple cheeseburger, large fries, and chocolate milkshake you're craving aren't exactly heart-friendly fare! Believe me, when it comes to angelic advice, nothing is off-limits. It's also common to be startled—or scared you-know-what-less—by their surprise visits. But they certainly don't hold their breath, eager to shout, "Three strikes... you're out!" and boot us from the plate.

Angels—especially those who work closely with humans, like archangels and guardian angels—are rooting for us. They reach out, not to smack us down but to lift us up. They're always waiting in the wings (no pun intended) to catch us when we fall.

2

What Angels Do

Right about now, you might be wondering what angels—particularly those closest to us—do in the human world. The big-picture answer is ANYTHING THAT'S NECESSARY. A more detailed description would be as follows: their job and their joy is to help, heal, protect, advise, comfort, connect, infuse, and inspire us. Let's look at each in turn.

Help
Angels are ready and willing to help. However, we must ask them to do so.

Doreen Virtue affirms that there's a universal law which states that "no angel shall interfere with a human's life unless asked, with the sole exception of a life-threatening emergency." This law prevents the angels from interfering with free will.

And that goes for *everyone's* free will. If you beg the angels to make a certain someone fall in love with you, you're wasting your breath. Angels will respect that person's freedom as much as yours.

However, if you're worried about family or friends, you can definitely ask angels to surround and support them. The angels won't meddle or make choices for your loved one, but they will comfort and guide the individual and perhaps take the edge off a situation.

How do you ask angels for help? You can do it directly or—if you're more comfortable with traditional prayer—through God. Personally, I do both, yet the two aren't mutually exclusive. When you communicate with angels, you're also connecting with the universal mind (God), and vice versa.

Above all, don't be intimidated by the whole affair. Doreen Virtue's maxim is that God and the angels aren't complicated, and it's truer than you might think. In fact, angels are just as simple or complex as we ourselves make them.

There's no need to memorize scores of hard-to-pronounce names unless you truly want to do so. As D. J. Conway explains in *Guides, Guardians, and Angels*, you can simply ask for the Angel of Parking Spaces, for example, or the Angel of Easy Travel, the Angel of Finding the Right Help, and so forth.

In chapters 4 and 5, we'll discuss how to connect and communicate with angels in more detail. For now, just know that angels can help with a variety of issues.

A friend of mine longed to give her daughter the nicest wedding possible, but she and her husband weren't sure how they'd foot the bill. She prayed for assistance. Soon thereafter, while standing outside of her car at a highway rest stop, something told her to look down. On the ground in front of her was a pill bottle. She scooped it up and removed the lid to find not pills, but a substantial sum of money. She was certain an angel had guided her to find it.

In *Praying with Angels*, Richard Webster gives the example of Pope Pius XI (1857–1939), who reportedly prayed to his guardian angel twice a day. If Pius suspected someone would reject his ideas during an upcoming meeting, he asked his guardian angel to speak with that person's guardian angel beforehand to ensure a harmonious encounter.

Of course, help isn't just about getting what we want. Sometimes angels assist us by placing obstacles in our paths. Your car breaks down for no apparent reason but does so at the perfect place and time for you to see an amazing spectacle or to help someone else. A vivid nightmare makes you grateful for the blessings you already have. Circumstance or a premonition prevents you from catching your flight, which then crashes and leaves no survivors.

What about the passengers who make the flight? Their conscious minds might be wholly unaware of the transition at hand, but their souls know. If it's their time to go, angels would remove any obstacles to boarding that airplane.

If it's not your "time," you won't go! I need only consult my family tree as proof. While still in Ireland, my great-grandfather's brother missed his boat to America—the *Titanic*—then made it over unscathed on the *Lusitania*.

Healing

Every one of us has needed or will need healing in all its forms: physical, emotional, mental, and spiritual. Angels excel in this area. In fact, the well-known author, psychic, and leading Theosophist Geoffrey Hodson (1886–1983) listed Angels of Healing as one of the seven primary groups of angels in existence, along with Angels of Power, Guardian Angels of the Home, Builder Angels, Angels of Nature, Angels of Music, and Angels of Beauty and Art. These healing angels, headed by Archangel Raphael, can help you maintain good health, overcome addictions, and recover from an illness or injury.

Healing angels are everywhere, not just in hospitals and doctors' offices. Like all angels, they fly to your side the instant you ask for their assistance, often before you've finished saying or thinking the words. Just last week, I silently called on Raphael to heal my lower back. A second later, my seven-year-old son, Geoffrey, asked why he was seeing a green light—a color associated with that archangel and with healing in general—then proceeded to speak to the angel he called "Ralph."

All angels can help with the healing process, and they often aid psychic and spiritual healers, whose patients report feeling an overwhelming, almost tangible sense of love or another set of hands on them during the healing session. Eight years ago, I experienced this phenomenon myself when a woman who was being trained in energy work practiced on me. At times, I was certain she was touching one part of my body only to discover she was focusing on a different, often distant spot. When I mentioned it to her, she concluded it was one of the many angels she'd sensed assisting her with my healing. I didn't doubt her word, for the sensations felt as warm and solid as an actual hand on my flesh.

During one of our sessions, she giggled suddenly. "Whoa," she said. "Okay."

She rarely spoke while working, so I opened my eyes. "What is it?" I asked.

"Something big just stepped in my way: an angel," she said. "My hands were the usual distance from your body, but it lifted them higher. I wasn't sure at first, so I tried to lower them. Then it moved them up again and pushed me backwards. The angel must know something I don't. I'd better keep my hands where it wants them."

Two weeks later, I learned I was pregnant. Soon after, a Reiki master explained to me that when a woman is pregnant, it's best to surround her body with an energetic, protective bubble and work around it. The angel who guided the other energy worker must've shared this view and resolved to protect my body's precious cargo.

Protection

"For he shall give his angels charge over thee, to keep thee in all thy ways. They shall bear thee up in their hands, lest thou dash thy foot against a stone." (Psalms 91: 11–12)

Each one of us has a guardian angel (more on this subject in chapter 6), but there are other angels who serve in this capacity. In general, the more challenges we face, the more angels there are who look out for us. The greater the problem, the greater the power of the angels involved. In *Phenomenon: Everything You Need to Know About the Paranormal*, Sylvia Browne asserts that these greater numbers or levels of angels are chosen for us before we're even born and are expressly related to the goals and experiences we plan for ourselves ahead of time.

A number of archangels are associated with protection. Archangel Michael is well known as the go-to angel when fear or danger threaten us. Archangel Ariel protects animals and the environment. Besides his healing activities, Archangel Raphael protects travelers.

I strongly suspect Raphael kept an eye on my mother during her recent trip to Peru. She, my father, and their tour group were in the town below Machu Picchu, preparing to visit the ruins, when her foot jammed into a sidewalk curb. Airborne from the impact, she flew forward.

Time seemed to stop but several thoughts sped through her mind.

I've really done it this time. I'm going to land on my head, and it's going to be really bad. What if I die? Who will take care of Bill [her husband]? There's so much I want to say to my kids.

Suddenly, a wave of peace washed over her, and a message flooded her mind: *THIS WON'T TURN INTO A TRAGEDY.*

She sensed that a number of angels guided her body and cushioned her fall. Then she landed directly on her knees. The tourists who witnessed her unscheduled "flight" feared she wouldn't come out of the accident well, if at all. Yet, despite considerable pain, my mother managed to fulfill her childhood dream of climbing the ruins that day. She has since described Machu Picchu as the most spiritual place she's ever visited.

Protection isn't just for the body; it applies to every aspect of the human experience, including our mental and emotional states. The flip side of Archangel Michael's warrior persona is his role as "the protector of joy." He can clear away any negativity, outer or inner. Doreen Virtue's description of this type of energy exchange (negative for positive) matches up with something my son Geoffrey perceived late one night when he was five.

I was in a foul mood that night, so I asked Michael to suck the negativity from my body and replace it with positive energy. A few minutes later, a noise from my sons' bedroom sent me down the hall and into the bright light of their bathroom, where Geoffrey stood waiting for me. I half-kneeled, half-sat in front of him.

He moved his gaze to the top of my head and all the way up to the ceiling, at which point his eyes widened. "Somebody else is here too," he said.

Someone tall, by the looks of it.

"No, I don't want to be happy," he said, frowning.

Then he gently hit the top of my head three times with the palm of his hand. "Now I want to be happy," he concluded.

In the space of fifteen seconds, he'd summed up the energy transfer that was taking place. The archangel—or one of his comrades—was literally "sucking out" the darkness from my crown chakra (the topmost energy vortex within the human frame) and replacing it with light.

Advice

There's a reason why the words for "angel" in various languages derived from—or are the same as—the term "messenger." They are indeed divine messengers. As such, they *advise* us in both senses of the word: they can inform us of events or situations and recommend actions that will benefit us and everyone involved.

One morning, a good friend of mine was lying in bed when without warning, an otherworldly voice told her that her youngest daughter had cancer. Thankfully, it hastened to add that the little girl would be all right. Subsequent medical tests confirmed the news, and treatments began right away.

During those treatments, the girl observed what she called "rainbow people." They floated in the air—a few feet off the ground—and looked like thirty-something humanoids glowing in a rainbow of colors. The sight of them was both comforting and commonplace, for they also appeared to her and to her grandmother at home. They even advised her when to stay home from school, safeguarding her health every step of the way.

Today, she's a beautiful, healthy woman. She's never forgotten the rainbow people who stood by her side, and her mother is beyond grateful to the heavenly helper who disclosed not only the cancer, but the eventual cure.

Comfort

All angels can comfort us in our darkest moments, but some are acknowledged as masters in the art. Archangel Cassiel is known as the Angel of Solitude and Tears. He's a quiet, calm presence who cares deeply for humanity and lessens the suffering—of both immediate family and the masses—caused by the death of monarchs and other rulers. He can also share the burden of our personal sorrows.

Archangel Raphael eases all forms of pain: physical, mental, emotional, and spiritual. He also keeps a special eye on people who comfort and heal others. One of my friends is a gifted healer. Several years back, when she was going through a difficult divorce and custody situation, she had an encounter with an angelic being she suspects was Raphael. She awoke one night around 3:00 a.m. to a buzzing sound and glimpsed a large, green "angel figure" at the foot of her bed. Its emanation of unconditional love was so powerful that she felt the energy long after the apparition faded. She believes he appeared to let her know that there was support from the Other Side and he'd be by her side through the tough times ahead.

When personal comfort is thwarted because we fail to forgive ourselves or others, Archangel Zadkiel is "the angel with the angle." He can help you release judgment—of big things or small—and fill your heart with compassion.

Connection

Believe it or not, connecting with angels is a natural ability, which we'll discuss in chapter 4. But it's not just about connection with them. Angels foster our sense of unity with everyone and everything in creation, and ultimately, with God. They pull out all the stops to expand our vision and help us notice the incredible interconnection of our universe. Take, for example, the angelically orchestrated details surrounding the birth of my children.

Dreams and a number of signs revealed my monozygotic twin pregnancy long before the doctors had a clue. Even when the ultrasound confirmed it, the babies' sex remained a mystery. They were simply Baby A (from my perspective, on the right side of my growing abdomen) and Baby B (on the left), and apparently, babies never switch sides during a twin pregnancy. My husband, Dan, and I decided on four names, two for boys and two for girls. If the babies were boys, the one on my right would be Connor; the left one would be Geoffrey.

When Dan announced the names to his mother, her response was instantaneous. "They're going to be boys," she said.

The reason for her certainty? In the office where she worked, the coworker on her right had a child named Connor and the one on her left had a child named Geoffrey.

During my seventh month of pregnancy, the boys wanted OUT, so I went into premature labor. I called my parents, who lived more than a thousand miles away, right after my water broke that morning and didn't contact them again until after the births. Half an hour before my emergency C-section, about which they knew nothing, they went out to dinner.

A short while into their meal, a toddler at the next table let out a single cry. He'd been calm and well-behaved before then, and his cry sounded more like an infant's.

Suddenly, my mother knew. *One of the babies was just born*, she thought.

She asked my father to check his watch for the time. It was 6:15 p.m.

One minute later, the same child emitted a second cry, which also resembled an infant's. My dad glanced at his watch again. It read 6:16 p.m.

"There goes the second one," my mother said.

The toddler kept quiet for the rest of the meal. First thing after dinner, my mom called Dan on his cell phone, and he confirmed the twins had arrived.

"What time were they born?" she asked.

It came as no surprise when he answered, "6:15 and 6:16."

What did surprise all of us was a related phenomenon. Three women who were knitting blankets for the boys stayed up most of the previous night to complete them. Even though the due date was six weeks away, a sense of urgency—i.e., an angelic nudge—compelled them to finish the job.

Our angels communicate with each other, and their combined efforts create a network of phenomenal precision and power. That synchronicity reminds us that there's more going on than our five senses suppose. Everyone and everything is connected.

Infusion

Psychologists, philosophers, and mystics have long contemplated the "peak experience," a miraculous, euphoric moment when a person transcends material illusion and perceives universal harmony or a "higher truth." It occurs suddenly and might follow intense feelings of love, deep meditation, or exposure to great art, literature, music, or natural beauty. I believe that most peak experiences are infusions of divine energy, facilitated by angels. When I was eight years old, I had one.

I was sitting in my third-grade classroom when all of a sudden, a peculiar urge struck me.

I want to be like Jesus for the rest of the day, I thought. *I will be love.*

That desire created an immediate reaction in my body. My scalp began to tingle, and the sensation traveled down my spine and out into my limbs. I felt "light," for lack of a better word, as if I hovered above my chair. I gazed at the books, the table, and the graceful clouds drifting beyond exquisitely crafted windowpanes. All seemed alive, composed of a million tiny, shimmering particles. Nothing around me seemed solid. I stared at the pencil in my hand and perceived no true separation between the instrument and my fingers. As I turned to observe both students and teacher, I was overcome by the realization we were all connected, each an extension of the other, every one of us part of some grand whole.

If you're a movie buff, picture the scene from *The Matrix* in which Keanu Reeves's character, Neo, finally sees and comprehends the true nature of the matrix, and you'll have some idea of what I experienced. No numbers or neon green during my big moment, but it forever shifted my view of the universe.

Angels can also facilitate infusions of knowledge: downloads from the akashic records, a.k.a. the universal supercomputer or the Mind of God. *Akasha* or *akash* is the Sanskrit word for "ether" (an invisible substance within and around every atom in the universe), and the akashic records are the sum total of all information—

pertaining to the history/experience of the universe
and all of its inhabitants—recorded on that substance.
In *Phenomenon*, Sylvia Browne describes that information as "imprinted on the ether of every planet, solar
system, and galaxy God created." She goes on to explain
that the akashic records also exist in written form in the
Other Side's Hall of Records. Many believe Archangel
Metatron is its master librarian.

The term "akashic record" originated with Theosophy, a spiritual philosophy which merges the world's
religious, philosophical, and scientific beliefs into a
unified world view. Its most visible proponent was the
nineteenth-century psychic and mystic, Helena Blavatsky. The term was later popularized by the remark-
able psychic Edgar Cayce, but correlations can be found
in the Hindu philosophy of *Samkhya,* the Buddhist concept of *alaya-vijnana,* the Australian Aboriginal Dreamtime, and the Matrix of remote viewing.

The "download" of data from this universal record
happens abruptly, and the information is specific. Suddenly, you just *know* something, and there's no logical
reason why you should.

Here's an example. When my maternal grandfather's naval ship sank during World War II, my grandmother received word he'd been killed in action. She
ignored the telegram and remained calm, but not out
of denial. She simply knew her husband was alive, that
it wasn't his "time." Months later, that knowledge was

vindicated, and the two of them spent the next sixty-three years together.

The akashic records are real, and so are infusions from its store. As Chantel Lysette explains in *The Angel Code*, "It's like pulling information straight out of thin air. In actuality, you're connecting with Archangel Metatron, or his library assistant Archangel Ramiel, who allow you access to the most comprehensive database in all of Creation."

Inspiration

In physiological terms, inspiration is drawing air into the lungs. Mental and spiritual inspiration—the "breaths" of the soul—are every bit as important to life as we know it, and life as we wish it to be.

I can't take full credit for what I write; so much of it seems a co-creation. I'd have to be naïve or egocentric not to suspect angelic input, because I feel exquisitely close to God while writing. People from all walks of life and every profession are inspired to do *whatever* they do in unique ways. Being "in the zone" is not only possible, but probable, especially with angels on your side. And they are literally at your side—at least one of them is right this instant!

Often, we're inspired to take specific actions. During World War II, my grandfather (mentioned above) and one other man were sitting in their ship's radio room when two kamikaze planes crashed into the vessel. The entire destroyer sank in three minutes, so there wasn't much time to think and only two portholes through which to escape. The other man—whose surname was identical to my grandfather's—chose the nearest porthole and ended up dying. But my grandfather, who had never learned to swim, heard a forceful, inner voice that told him to use the other porthole. He jumped through it and landed in the water near an ammunition can. With fire all around him, he clung to that can and dodged bullets from Japanese planes overhead for twelve hours before his eventual rescue. Clearly, it wasn't his day to die, and at least one angel played a role.

Miracles big and small happen every day. Think of those dark moments when you felt you couldn't go on, only to receive a sudden jolt of "Oh yes, I can!" Or the impulse to give a homeless man a ten-dollar bill, instead of loose change. Remember the problem that plagued you at bedtime and the perfect solution that struck you upon waking.

Don't get me wrong. Human compassion and ingenuity—as well as our indomitable spirits—are certainly capable of creating these phenomena. But during such moments, the angels love and support us so we can act from our highest selves. And chances are, at one time or another, the magic wand of angelic inspiration has tapped us all.

3

Archangels

An arch spans a distance while supporting a weight above it, as in a bridge or a doorway. Angels of the "arch" variety serve a similar purpose. They bridge the perceived gap between humans and the divine while supporting the source of creation. They provide a doorway to understanding by reminding us of our highest visions of ourselves. They also supervise vast numbers of other angels, and as you probably gathered from the previous chapter, specialize in certain functions.

In Jungian psychology, archetypes are images from the collective unconscious: inherited, universal symbols that inhabit the "messenger field" of the human mind. They crop up in dreams, myths, personalities, etc., but no matter where or how they appear, they enrich the human experience. So do archangels.

As we'll discuss in chapter 5, divine messengers communicate with us in a variety of ways, including dreams and meditative visions. Whatever the method of contact, archangels can present—or take the form of—specific animals and often use symbols to clue us in on their identity. Following my individual descriptions of archangels, I'll give you the animals and symbols associated with each of them. They're common associations, together with several listed in Chantel Lysette's *The Angel Code*.

Ultimately, the angels will work with you to develop a unique symbology that makes sense to you. In the meantime, you can use the information in this chapter as a foundation upon which to build.

How Many Archangels Are There?

Their number is still debated and, like the spelling of their names, depends largely on your source material. According to Judeo-Christian and Western mystery traditions, there are four superstars: Michael (meaning of name: "Who is like God"), Gabriel ("Might of God"), Raphael ("God's healing"), and Uriel ("Fire/Light of God"). Here's a rundown of each.

Michael

Michael is a leader among the archangels; some say he's *the* leader. Traditionally, he's the patron angel of police officers, firefighters, and all who preserve truth and justice.

He also supports so-called "lightworkers": humans—teachers, healers, authors, artists, etc.—inspired to help the world through spiritual energy. He can remove blockages of any type, and his top priority is protecting the planet and its inhabitants from negativity, particularly the energy of fear and anything associated with it. Believe me, he can clean house like nobody's business!

He's also the "Mr. Fix-It" of the angelic realm and is especially sharp when electrical or mechanical devices are involved. Turning to Michael when your computer rebels might seem sacrilegious or downright ridiculous, but what have you got to lose?

Joan of Arc asserted that Archangel Michael guided her actions and gave her courage. Apparently, he first appeared to her in 1424 when she was just twelve years old. Archangel Gabriel made an appearance too.

Some perceive Michael's light as red, but blue and purple are also associated with him. Personally, I see purple sparkles and flashes of bright blue when he's around—although on rare occasions, a hint of red emerges—and the colors are always accompanied by a huge shift in air pressure. His commanding presence is unmistakable, and his calling card is a fierce, warm energy that inspires an immediate sense of courage, strength, and conviction. And just so you know, I'm not on any medications!

A few years ago, I encountered Michael while resting alone in bed. Sparks of purple light danced behind my closed eyelids. The next instant, the color shifted into the most intense blue I'd ever seen and shaped it-self into a solid orb.

"What is this?" I said aloud. I almost opened my eyes but thought better of it and amended my question. "Who are you?"

The orb became an eye, surrounded by—and seemingly composed of—fire, not unlike the image of the all-seeing eye depicted in Peter Jackson's *The Lord of the Rings* film trilogy. But my vision differed from the movie version in two key ways: 1. the flames in and around the eye were blue; and 2. I felt no fear, only awe.

The image was as striking as it was startling. I moved to sit up, but something pressed my shoulders back against the bed. A heartbeat later, a roaring force I can only describe as a "cosmic wind" rushed over my body. It lasted for maybe a minute. Then all was calm, and I was floating above my bed, pulled by an unseen force toward the nearest wall.

I passed through the wall with ease, and then sound supplanted sight. A constant flow of noise drifted toward me from seemingly every house in the neighborhood: whispered prayers, phone conversations, news broadcasts, and the lilting laughter of children playing.

Of two things I was positive: a larger, protective spirit was with me, and it was trustworthy. I questioned my companion about a long-cherished goal. The answer was loud and clear:

PATIENCE.

The cosmic wind returned, but not for long. All at once, it ceased and a thunderclap sliced the air. I was back in bed. My entire body vibrated, so I opened my eyes to make sure it was all in one piece. When the sensation passed, I rolled out of bed and headed toward the computer for a little research.

Before long, I found two intriguing clues to my experience. First, the cosmic wind and thunderclap were linked with spirit visitations and astral travel. For those unfamiliar with the term, astral travel is an out-of-body experience during which one sometimes experiences both the journey and the destination. (More on astral travel in chapter 9.) Second, Archangel Michael was associated with the "Blue Flame of the Will of God" and the "Blue Lightning of Cosmic Christ Protection," and his eyes were sometimes described as pools of fire.

The fiery blue eye that I encountered felt so powerful and so profound, I knew I was in the presence of something sacred. Now, after numerous encounters, I recognize that telltale energy as Michael's.

In conventional images, Michael sports armor and brandishes a sword, and I asked him if he was really the warrior he's made out to be.

YES AND NO, he answered. *I DON'T SMITE THE WICKED, BUT I HAVE A FIERCE ENERGY THAT HOLDS SWAY OVER MOST ANY SITUATION. MY REPUTATION AS A WARRIOR IS REALLY STRENGTH OF CONVICTION MISINTERPRETED.*

Animals: bear, bull, cardinal, cock, eagle, falcon, hawk, lion

Symbols: blue flame, chain mail, flag, javelin, medieval suit of armor, scales (of justice), shield, sword

Gabriel

The Bible says that Archangel Gabriel went to Nazareth and told Mary she'd bear a son named Jesus. The Qur'an also describes the event: "We sent to her Our angel, and he appeared before her as a man in all respects." (the Chapter of Mary 19:17) According to Muslim scripture, that same Gabriel (Jibril) dictated the word of God (Allah) to Muhammad. He's a messenger in the truest sense of the word.

As such, he can help you receive and understand any message from Spirit, be it from God, a spirit guide, or your deceased Aunt Bertha. He can also assist your efforts to send messages, particularly those of a spiritual nature. It's little wonder that he's regarded as the angel of guidance, as well as the patron angel of human messengers. It doesn't matter whether you're a writer, reporter, radio personality, motivational speaker, master of the internet, actor, musician, or dancer; if you're involved in communication or the arts, Gabriel knows about it.

In addition, Gabriel has a hand in new beginnings, which can definitely occur with the conception or adoption of a child. He lends courage and strength to parents, and speaking as a parent, we need it! Furthermore, if you're an artist—storyteller, poet, painter, sculptor, or what have you—and think of your creations as children, Gabriel has your back.

Some say his light is blue. Others connect his energy with orange, copper, or gold. Not surprising when you consider the recurring image of his horn, although I prefer to think of it not as a trumpet but as an open telephone line of communication; "on the horn" with God, so to speak. Still, well before I learned his identity, Gabriel appeared to me in those very colors.

One night, a decade ago, I lay in bed listening to my husband's inimitable snore. I stared into the darkness that should've been the ceiling. It seemed alive with a zillion particles darting this way and that.

Suddenly, a light appeared high above the foot of the bed. It expanded into a wraithlike figure whose color was a blend of orange and gold. The vibe of this "light being" was definitely feminine; of course, I now know it was just one aspect of good old Gabriel. His arms moved with ethereal grace, and his long hair and garment floated on the air, as if he were immersed in water or had his own wind machine.

At first, his presence seemed as natural and predictable as rain in the spring. I knew he was supposed to be there, and although I couldn't fathom his purpose, I sensed nothing but infinite love. So I just went with the moment, and inexplicably chalked it up to a vision or a waking dream.

What a beautiful image, I thought.

Then Gabriel drifted closer and shifted into a horizontal pose, mirroring my position on the bed.

My scalp tingled. My heart thumped in my chest.

Without a word, he descended toward me. I expected him to stop, but the gap between us was closing fast and a little too close for comfort. Only an arm's length away, he continued to advance.

Wait a minute, I thought. *This isn't a dream. I'm awake!*

He surged right up to my face, and I flinched against my pillow. The next instant, he vanished.

I thrust my hands into the air above me. There was nothing. Not a single trace to verify my encounter.

Nevertheless, my train of thought was both conscious and continuous throughout the experience, and I was strangely out of sorts when I woke the next morning. I felt like I was standing at the edge of a cliff, poised to plummet into the abyss. Clearly, my soul was privy to some impending horror.

The visitation occurred one week before I embarked on a little journey Dan and I refer to as the Year From Hell. During that period, frustration over delays to my role as an author or "messenger" manifested as a chronic, excruciating physical condition I wouldn't wish on anyone. Gabriel knew that storm was coming. I believe he warned me about it, or reminded me of it, and attempted to reassure me that the strength of God—the actual definition of his name—would see me through.

Animals: chameleon, giraffe, grasshopper, gull, hawk, horse, rhinoceros, robin, sparrow, starling

Symbols: banner, lily, paintbrush, pen, quill and inkwell, scroll, sword, trumpet (or any horn)

Raphael

Raphael plays a pivotal role in the apocryphal book of Tobit, which is still included in the Catholic Bible, and is sometimes called the angel of compassion. It stands to reason because he's the patron angel of anyone in the business of healing: doctors, nurses, pharmacists, herbalists, chiropractors, therapists of every sort, acupuncturists, medical intuitives, shamans, yoga instructors, and practitioners of all forms of energy work. If you're passionate about the healing arts, Raphael will ensure that the training you need, as well as the finances to support it, will manifest.

If you or a loved one—including animals—need physical, mental, emotional, or spiritual healing, call on Raphael. You might receive hands-on healing from the archangel himself, which can feel like a tingling sensation in the area of concern. Or he might facilitate an appointment with the perfect doctor, in whose ear he'll whisper the best treatment. Even when physical healing remains at bay, Raphael can heal us on other levels, and he can help those struggling with addictions.

By the way, archangels do work together. Disease (the body's dis-ease) is often rooted in negativity, so a little teamwork from Raphael and Michael can work wonders. Raphael also has a special interest in science—especially astronomy—and travel. Whether you're a routine traveler, globetrotter, or once-in-a-lifetime tourist, Raphael can smooth the way.

Some say his vibrations come in shades of violet. He can also be seen as flashes or sparkles of emerald green light.

A few years ago, I had a splitting headache for four days straight. It affected only the left side of my head for two of those days. I must've looked like hell, because on the morning of the third day, my son Connor—then three years old—approached me with wide, compassionate eyes.

"Don't worry, Mommy," he said, grabbing my hand. "I fix it."

He pulled me off my chair and had me kneel in front of him. The next thing I knew, he was tapping his fingers on the top of my head. He uttered short, specific sounds which bore no resemblance to English or any other language I've studied and intoned different notes with each tap. I got the strange impression he viewed my head as a computer.

After about a minute, he stopped. So did the pain.

I gazed into his beautiful brown eyes, and he gave me a little smile. "All better now," he said. Then he ran back to his brother's side to play.

Five minutes later, the headache returned, but from that point on it affected only the right side of my head. I thought of something a Reiki Master once told me: "The left side of the body corresponds to the subconscious, and the right side represents the conscious mind."

Had Connor shifted the energy of pain—presumably a blockage of some sort—from my subconscious to my conscious mind, in order for it to be healed? Was it possible that the archangels Raphael and Michael guided his actions?

Instinct told me to phone a BodyTalk practitioner who'd assisted me before. For those who've never heard of BodyTalk, it's a form of therapy which aims to harmonize the body's interactive network of energy matrixes, bringing balance to the body so it can resume normal operations.

As soon as I mentioned the headache, the practitioner had an answer. "Stuff from a past life has come to the surface so you can let it go."

Without warning, the air pressure changed, and my head, shoulders, and arms tingled as though they'd received a soft, warm caress. Someone invisible had joined me in the room.

"Three angels are going to be helping you with this," the practitioner continued. "Archangels Michael and Raphael are coming in to work with your guardian angel. Can you feel them?" Mind you, I'd said nothing to her about angels, "arch" or otherwise.

She did her thing on her end and talked me through a series of touches—some strong and sustained, others gentle and fleeting—which I performed to the best of my ability. When I hung up the phone ten minutes later,

I felt remarkably better. By the end of the day, the headache was history, and I was incredibly thankful for Raphael's assistance.

Animals: cat, deer, dolphin, dove (white), dragonfly, duck, fish, frog, horse, owl, rabbit, snake, whale, wolf, unicorn

Symbols: mortar and pestle, shepherd's staff, sun

Uriel

Archangel Uriel has received a bum rap in some quarters. In his defense, I must say that he, too, is an expression of God's infinite love. When I asked him about his harsh reputation, he answered immediately.

PEOPLE SEE ANGELS THROUGH THEIR PERSONAL FILTERS. IN AN ATTEMPT TO HUMANIZE, THEY PROJECT HUMAN FOIBLES ONTO US. IN TRUTH, I AM ALL-LOVING, AS ARE MY BROTHER ANGELS.

Like a quiet sage hovering in the background, Uriel is the embodiment of the phrase "Still waters run deep." He's been called the Prince of Knowledge and Truth, the Archangel of Prophecy, the Archangel of Transformation, and the great harmonizer of substance within and between each body. He imparts great wisdom and insight, supports intellectual and spiritual growth, and encourages contemplation and "deep" conversations. He illuminates dark places—whether they're inside or outside of us—to bring understanding.

Many believe that Uriel helps us deal with natural disasters and earth changes and that it was he who warned Noah of the imminent flood. He's also supposed to have given the Kabbalah and alchemy to mankind. A variety of colors are associated with him: pale yellow, gold, red, brown, black, and silver.

The night before I started this section, I lay in bed and called on Uriel…in my mind, of course; I didn't want to wake my husband. Immediately, a yellow glow appeared mere inches from my face. Within seconds, it turned to gold.

I guess that's you, I thought. *I have the feeling you've always been around me, but our relationship hasn't seemed very experiential. I need your help, because I want to paint a picture of you that's as accurate as possible. I'm open to whatever you'd like to show me.*

The next instant, a riot of silver-white lights twinkled above me, like sequins on black velvet. I felt as if I was stargazing and each "star" symbolized some nugget of knowledge or spark of divinity. Suddenly, they drifted downward, resembling snowflakes on a calm night. When they were about two feet away, the "flakes" transformed into small, white feathers. Then, with a sudden burst of air, they blew right into my face. I closed my eyes just in time and experienced the impact as a dozen tiny prickles on my cheeks and forehead.

I opened my eyes. There was no sign of feathers, but the pale, yellow glow was back, hovering about a foot above my head.

I could almost hear the words, *HOW'S THAT FOR EXPERIENTIAL?*

Not bad.

Animals: boar, lizard, phoenix, ram, rhinoceros, snow leopard

Symbols: bow and arrow, chariot, flaming whip, lightning, open hand holding a flame, scroll, scales (of justice), torch

The "Big Four"—Michael, Gabriel, Raphael, and Uriel—are the celebrities of angelic lore, so it's only natural that word of mouth and the power of the press gravitate to them. There are also a number of other archangels, lesser known but just as important. Here are some of them.

Ariel

Ariel guards the balance of nature and is mentioned in a number of mystical texts, including the Book of Ezra, whose earliest version dates to around 400 BCE, and *The Key of Solomon the King*, translated from ancient manuscripts in 1889. He works with Archangels Chamuel and Raphael to heal humans, animals, and plants and is especially involved in purifying and protecting bodies of water. In *Archangels and Ascended Masters*, Doreen Virtue states that Ariel supervises the nature spirits known as sprites and works closely with Solomon, who's now an ascended master. (More on ascended masters in chapter 7.)

Animals: all creatures but lion in particular, as well as bear, cheetah, hawk, horse, raven, zebra

Symbols: javelin, jewels, sword and shield, water, wind

Azrael

Better known as the Angel of Death, Azrael is described as a tall, dark, quiet, and composed archangel responsible for releasing souls from their physical bodies at the moment of death. In one of alternative healing's core texts, *Hands of Light*, the gifted healer Barbara Brennan describes Azrael as "strong and beautiful," not scary at all. She tells of an encounter that occurred when she helped a woman who'd been ill for quite a while and was two days from death. Apparently, the woman was out of her body—off with one of her spirit guides— most of the time, but at one point, she experienced terrible pain. Brennan glimpsed Azrael guarding the gate, and she asked him why he didn't help the woman die. He replied, "I haven't received my orders yet." With love and compassion, Azrael comforts the dying and the grieving. He also protects grief counselors from absorbing the brunt of their clients' sorrow. But Azrael doesn't appear just when death is near. He helps people who are afraid of death or the unknown overcome their fears, and as Richard Webster affirms in *Encyclopedia of Angels*, Azrael also aids in the exploration of past lives.

Animals: bat, beetle, butterfly, crow, dragon, moth, raven, vulture

Symbols: bridge, scythe, skeleton, skull, veil

Cassiel

As the Angel of Solitude and Tears, Cassiel lends his quiet, reassuring presence to those burdened by sorrow. Some know him as the Angel of Temperance. He can help humans develop patience, overcome setbacks, and conquer long-standing difficulties. He's also linked with karma and helps people comprehend the Law of Cause and Effect. Francis Barrett's *The Magus*, published in 1801, contains a well-known illustration of Cassiel with a dark beard and a crown atop his head. He's riding a dragon and gripping an arrow with his right hand. In *The Angel Code*, Chantel Lysette describes him clad like a member of a goth rock band. She states that many of her clients who encountered Cassiel in the dream state believed they were seeing ghosts, vampires, or werewolves, although none felt threatened in any way. She explains, "This is Cassiel's *modus operandi*—to use his appearance as a way of letting us know that exteriors mean little in the grander scheme of things." Cassiel puts me in mind of the musical *The Phantom of the Opera*, particularly the song "The Music of the Night," with the night symbolizing any darkness we might experience. Cassiel helps us shoulder the shadows and find the inherent beauty—however well it's hidden—in feeling the entire spectrum of human emotions.

Animals: crow, dragon, koi (ornamental varieties of carp), raven, snow leopard, snowy owl, sparrow, spider, vulture

Symbols: arrow, crown, full moon, graveyard, sword

Chamuel

Chamuel, also known as Camael, supervises the order and balance of nature and is deeply invested in world peace. He helps humans understand and strengthen their relationships with each other and with planet Earth. He can also encourage willpower and perseverance within us and open doors to a more fulfilling career. Chamuel also opens our hearts to love—*true love*—not the flashy, fleeting imitation, but the real deal. Hence, as D. J. Conway asserts in *Guides, Guardians, and Angels*, Chamuel can help us find a suitable mate. Richard Webster advises in his *Encyclopedia of Angels* that we call on this angel for added strength, especially when conflicts arise in our relationships. Doreen Virtue and Chantel Lysette describe Chamuel as sweet, tranquil, and mild-mannered.

Animals: all animals, but especially goat, praying mantis, stag

Symbols: bamboo staff, gate, lotus, sword

Haniel

Haniel, also known as Anael, shares God's love and grace with us, no matter what circumstances we face, and he can boost our self-confidence. He can also help us expand our natural healing abilities and awaken our psychic senses, especially clairvoyance. Haniel has worked with humans for eons, and his movements are described as smooth and elegant. He has the energy of a moon goddess, defined by Doreen Virtue in *Archangels and Ascended Masters* as "etheric, quiet, patient, and mystical."

Animals: deer, dove, sparrow

Symbols: angel wings, crystals, heart, rainbow, sunbeams

Jophiel

Also known as Iophiel, this archangel is the patron of artists—whether they work with colors, textures, words, or musical notes—and anyone employing creative skills. He encourages us to appreciate the beauty within and around us. He also inspires us with ideas and energy to complete our own creations. In addition, he reminds us that we all require breaks from the hectic pace of modern life in order to "smell the roses."

Animals: bee, bison (buffalo), cougar, cow, fox, frog, hummingbird, panther, parrot, peacock, sea lion, seal, swan, tiger

Symbols: quarterstaff, roses

Metatron

As previously mentioned, Metatron is the keeper of the akashic records; he's also been called "God's secretary." He encourages spiritual development—in adults and children—and can spark or broaden comprehension of sacred geometry. Sacred geometry delves into the cosmic significance of geometric forms and the philosophical and spiritual beliefs they've inspired; sacred universal patterns—seen in everything from a nautilus to a tesseract (the four-dimensional extension of a cube) to structures like temples, cathedrals, and mosques—reveal the mathematical order and holographic nature of the universe. Metatron loves children and is particularly concerned about boys and girls who fall within the autistic spectrum, or who are saddled with labels like ADD (Attention Deficit Disorder) and ADHD (Attention Deficit Hyperactivity Disorder). According to Doreen Virtue in *Archangels and Ascended Masters*, "he helps parents, educators, scientists, and health-care professionals find natural alternatives to Ritalin and other psychoactive medications."

Animals: ant, crane, elephant, goldfish, goose, kitten, mouse, ostrich, prairie dog, puppy, stork

Symbols: books, clouds, library, pen, rainbow, robe

Raguel

Sometimes called the Archangel of Justice and Fairness, Raguel is the underdog's champion, helping a person to feel more empowered and gain respect. Raguel also ensures that all the archangels work together like clockwork. He can strengthen one's faith, promote cooperation among members of families or groups, and even offer legal advice. Raguel is a great detector of dishonesty, and as D. J. Conway asserts in *Guides, Guardians, and Angels*, he can help us see beyond illusions.

Animals: antelope, camel, donkey, elephant, mouse, ox, roadrunner, swift

Symbols: books, quill and inkwell

Ramiel

Also known as Jeremiel, this archangel is described in a first-century Judaic text, 2 Baruch, as the angel "who presides over true visions." (2 Baruch 55:3) As such, he can help you understand psychic dreams, particularly those which foretell future events. He is, after all, Metatron's "assistant librarian" with full access to the akashic records. He's also known for helping souls who've recently crossed to the Other Side review their most recent lives. In *Phenomenon*, Sylvia Browne states that this life review happens in 3-D in a "scanning machine" she describes as a large dome of blue glass in the Hall of Wisdom. Inside that dome, we view every moment from the life we've just completed, hyperconscious of how our decisions affected everyone around us and how well or poorly we accomplished the goals we set before birth. The process is more about reflection and realization than about judgment, and Ramiel can help us evaluate our lives even before we cross over so we can make positive changes that will benefit everyone.

Animals: owl, squirrel, wood rat

Symbols: calendar, hourglass, sundial

Raziel

Raziel knows all of the secrets of the universe and how it runs. He can enlighten you on any topic you might ponder, from sacred geometry to quantum mechanics to the rules of manifestation (the appearance of—or spiritual practice of creating/attracting—one's needs and desires). He encourages people to "think outside the box" and develop original ideas, but his messages can be rather cryptic. In the *Encyclopedia of Angels*, Richard Webster describes him as wearing a gray robe, "which appears to be liquid, rather than solid." Likewise, in *The Angel Code*, Chantel Lysette sees him as a mysterious, cloaked figure that "lurks in the dreamscape, imparting bits of wisdom and glimpses of the esoteric." Having encountered Raziel in dreams, and once, as an apparition in the waking world, I agree with these descriptions, as well as Doreen Virtue's assessment of him as subtle, intelligent, and kind. He might be profound, but he's also pleasant.

Animals: chameleon, eel, fox, panther, raven, scorpion, snake, spider

Symbols: blade, dagger, cloak, key, keyhole, mist, smoke, veil

Sandalphon

The derivation of his name is unclear, but there are two educated guesses: it comes from the Greek *sandalion* ("sandal"), thus meaning "one who wears sandals"; or it is the Greek prefix *sym-/syn-* ("together") plus *adelphos* ("brother"), which approximates the meaning "co-brother." Indeed, Sandalphon is known as the twin brother of Archangel Metatron. Described as extremely tall—stretching from Earth to Heaven—he's said to be the head of the guardian angels and the carrier of human prayers to God. He's also in charge of all bird life, which seems in keeping with his cheerful, chipper disposition, and he appeals to one's inner child. In *The Angel Code*, Chantel Lysette writes, "This angel was one of the spiritual influences for the Roman god Cupid, so feelings of elation and everything being right with the world are not uncommon when encountering him."

Animals: all birds but especially canary, coyote, dog, otter, porcupine

Symbols: candy, games, harp, wrapped presents

Zadkiel

Considered the archangel of mercy, Zadkiel clears the heart chakra of emotional debris and helps us forgive ourselves and others. He encourages us to see past the superficial level of individual egos and behavioral blunders to the spark of divinity which lies within us all. In this way, he promotes compassion, tolerance, and acceptance. He can also enhance memory and promote abundance of every sort, including financial. Together with Archangel Michael, he negates negative energies.

Animals: camel, donkey, dove, elephant, goat, ox, sheep

Symbols: books, scroll, shepherd's staff, violet flame

You've probably noticed that most of the archangels' names end in "el." *El,* one of the Hebrew names for God, comes from a root word that means "might, strength, power" and is thought to derive from the Ugaritic term for god. When embedded in the names of archangels, it means "of God."

The archangels might have specific functions and detectable personalities, but when you get down to it, they're simply aspects of the primal source. We couldn't ask for a better bridge to connect and attune us to its wisdom and benevolent energy.

4

How to Connect
with Angels

It's time to discuss what I believe are the four essentials to connecting with angels and the four "enhancers" that will greatly improve your relationship—and increase the clarity of your communication—with angels, guardians, guides, and any other spirit with whom you'd like to connect. Let's get started.

Essential 1: Belief in Angels

Angels exist. Theosophist Geoffrey Hodson shared the perspective of an angel named Bethelda in *The Brotherhood of Angels and of Men*, first published in 1927. He met Bethelda while meditating on a hillside in Gloucestershire. The sky and his consciousness filled with the light of the angel's love and wisdom, revealing to Hodson information about angelic and human cooperation. Here's a smidgen of what Bethelda had to say:

> To every man and woman in every walk of life in the lower worlds, the angels come. Bearing their perfume, the aroma of eternal ecstasy, they would waken in the hearts of every man a craving for that everlasting bliss; would give to men the knowledge that they have a heavenly home, would show them in the mirror of the mind the reflection of their heavenly self—the vision of their own immortality ...

> Members of the angel hosts are hovering over the heads of all congregations, standing beside every priest; yet how often do they find themselves shut out by barriers upraised by human minds! Let priest and congregation alike throw open their minds to a recognition of our presence in their midst; soon, very soon, some will begin to hear the beating of our wings, to feel an added power in their work, and, later, an increasing happiness in their lives ...

> Our sphere of usefulness to God will be enlarged by sharing yours; your lives will be enriched, your world made glad by the inauguration of the brotherhood of angels and of men ...

> The first essential on your side is a belief in our existence ...

Essential 2: The Realization that Angels are Everywhere

If your vision of angels consists only of their flying loop-the-loops in some far-off "heaven," you might want to expand it a little—or a lot. Angels are everywhere. Indoors and outdoors. At the opera, the football game, and the waterpark. At work, at school, and at home. And yes, I've encountered them in the bathroom on several occasions.

With our hectic lifestyles, it's easy to forget that angels are all around us. That's why reminders of their presence are helpful. You can hang angel artwork in your home or place an angel statue in your garden. Angel figurines, books about angels, and music that sounds angelic or celestial are also popular. If you plan to communicate with angels on a regular basis, you can designate a "sacred space" in which to do it. Any place where you feel peaceful, safe, and close to the divine will work: a comfortable spot beneath your favorite oak tree, a rocking chair in a quiet corner, or an altar perfumed by flowers or incense and decorated with candles and crystals. The choice is yours.

However, angels don't require any of the above paraphernalia to connect with us. Nor do they insist on specific rituals, prayers, or meditations. Those are merely tools to help *us* feel connected and open to communication. At the end of the day, the real sacred space is inside of you, and you can "go" there any time and any place you wish.

Angels are around us no matter what. But, as Sylvia Browne points out in *Phenomenon*, the more open, giving, and spiritually aware we become, the greater the number of angels we attract.

Essential 3: Willingness to Connect and Communicate with Angels

Remember, connection and communication with angels isn't as complicated as it's often made out to be. Physical reminders of their presence, rituals, prayers, and specific meditations do work, but your willingness to know and develop a rapport with them is most important. Just like our relationships with humans, rapport strengthens the more time we spend with the angels. Talk to them as you would a friend, in good times and in bad. Angels can certainly help during a crisis, but if that's the only time you attempt contact, your fear and panic might drown out their messages of comfort. Why settle for mere acquaintance when friendship is at hand?

Chantel Lysette echoes this sentiment in *The Angel Code* and suggests inviting the archangels to parties and reunions. You can even include them in run-of-the-mill activities like watching movies. Before you know it, connecting with the angels will become second nature.

The information on angels might seem overwhelming at first, but don't stress over it. Using an angel's proper name is wonderful, but in a pinch, you can do as D. J. Conway suggested: for example, calling on the Angel of Easy Travel to help you. Richard Webster suggests asking your guardian angel to connect you with the right angel for the task at hand. Doreen Virtue teaches that once you ask for angelic help, the Law of Attraction—by which like attracts like, akin to a universal photocopier—kicks in and automatically draws to your side the angel(s) best suited to your current needs.

All of these methods work. So don't let the long names and various associations bog you down. The main thing is your willingness to connect.

Essential 4: Remembrance of Your True Self, Which is Spirit

Most of you know this already, but for some reason, many still freak out when they think about ghosts (still earthbound) or spirits (crossed over). Newsflash: all of us—living or "dead"—are Spirit. Yoda, the Grover-sounding, wisdom-expounding Jedi Master in the *Star Wars* saga said it best: "Luminous beings are we, not this crude matter." Yet we become so accustomed to our earthly, three-dimensional existence that we forget our true essence is Spirit.

Yes, you're currently attached to a body. Nevertheless, you're an immortal spirit, intimately and inextricably connected with the spirit world. That world—in which our angels, guardians, and guides live and move—is really just another dimension right alongside our own. Vibrational energy is the key to understanding the different dimensions and the reason why most people see ghosts more easily than they do angels and other spirits.

Everything—from molecules to subatomic quanta—vibrates because it's packed with energy. That's a science fact, by the way, not science fiction or a New Age notion. The higher the vibration, the higher the dimension. In general, it's easier to see things that vibrate closer to our own rate of vibration.

The best example of this principle involves a ceiling fan analogy. At a standstill, the fully visible blades of a ceiling fan represent our physical bodies, which vibrate at quite a low rate. Turn that fan on low, and the image of the blades wavers and starts to disappear. That's like ghosts, whose vibratory rate is higher than ours but still relatively low. Switch to medium speed, and the blades seem to vanish. That's like spirits, whose vibrations are higher still. High speed represents the highest vibration, at which angels function, completely invisible unless we raise our own vibrations—through meditation and/or increasing our spiritual awareness—or they slow down theirs and manifest in human form.

Just remember, we're spirits too. Our physical bodies might have limitations, but our spirits have limitless potential. What applies in the spiritual dimension also applies to us; it's just that under "normal" circumstances, we don't experience it, or we don't realize we're experiencing it.

Enter the paranormal, the spirit world of which you are a part. For our purposes, the most important facets of that world are the four enhancers I mentioned earlier. They are unconditional love, freedom, nonlinear time, and nonlocality of the spirit. They walk hand in hand, and once you "get" them, your whole view of angels, guardians, and guides—and your relationship with them—will expand.

Enhancer 1: Unconditional Love

Unconditional love means love *with no conditions*. This is the kind of love which emanates unceasingly from the source of creation. As extensions of that source, angels are constantly bathed in its warmth and brilliance, so all is well from their perspective. "The agony and the ecstasy" of the human condition—our joys and sorrows, our strength and frailty, our crazy antics and worst behaviors, even our most mundane moments—melt into a grand continuum embraced and sustained by the miracle of unconditional love.

Believe me, I can catalog my personality flaws and turn from a full-length mirror in sheer horror with the best of you. But the angels don't care about all of that, except in the sense that they're willing to help us release it so we can continue moving along our respective paths.

So don't worry that the angels won't love you because you're too this or too that, or because you've done something you or the world deems unforgiveable. When you communicate with them, be honest. They already know you—better than you could ever imagine—by your unique energy signature. You won't disappoint them, and they won't judge you. In truth, most people are harder on themselves than any being of light would ever be. Angels, guardians, and guides hold a loving viewpoint which is so pervasive that it blots out our mistakes and counterbalances all negativity, which ultimately allows us to recall and reclaim our true essence.

The least you need to know about unconditional love: your angels, guardians, and guides love you no matter what you've ever thought, said, or done, and they couldn't care less about your physical appearance. Relax and be yourself with them.

Enhancer 2: Freedom

In Neale Donald Walsch's *Conversations with God* (Book 3), "God" says, "Any attempt to restrict the natural expressions of love is a denial of the experience of freedom—and thus a denial of the soul itself. For the soul is freedom personified. God is freedom, by definition—for God is limitless and without restriction of any kind. The soul is God, miniaturized."

In *Manifest Your Destiny: the Nine Spiritual Principles for Getting Everything You Want*, Dr. Wayne W. Dyer states, "The universal spirit permeates all space and all that is manifested, and we are all a part of that... It cannot have 'favorites' if it is the root and support for everything and everyone. Lacking individuality, it cannot be in conflict with your desires. Being universal, it cannot be simply shut off from you."

Eternal, pervasive, unconditional love makes the world go round and allows the universe to expand as it will. Notice the last three words of the previous sentence. AS IT WILL.

AS *WE* WILL.

In saying that, I'm not ignoring what people call "God's will." Yet we're so much freer than most of us realize. We are free to perceive the world as we wish, to discover that it's both objective and subjective. We are free to cocreate our reality, to experience whatever our souls choose to experience.

That freedom of perception and creation is precisely why everyone and no one is 100 percent accurate when discussing spiritual matters, or *any* matter. We each have a personal filter through which we interpret the universe, and our focus determines our life's course. That's what sages and mystics throughout human history have reminded us: we live in the universe, but the entire universe also lives within us.

Look for the good, and you'll find it. Expect the bad, and it'll show up right on schedule. If you believe with all your heart that angels wear tutus, don't be surprised if— when they finally appear to you—they choose that costume to help you recognize them. If the mere thought of death terrifies you because you think you've earned a front-row seat in Hell, you could literally scare the hell *out of yourself* during a near death experience and suffer that illusion on the astral plane. Yet even the most stubborn individuals shed the illusion and move on thanks to angels like Azrael, Zadkiel, and the Powers.

But why put yourself through that? Our energetic source, a.k.a. God, would never require it. As Shakespeare wrote, "Love does not alter when it alteration finds." Any love other than the unconditional kind is a cheap imitation.

Free will is the supreme expression of unconditional love and an unreturnable gift. It's so sacred that angels, guardians, and guides won't violate it. They make suggestions and work behind the scenes, but they never choose for us. And unless we ask for help—directly or through prayer—ascended masters and angels won't intervene, except in the case of angelic rescue from a premature death.

What are we doing with all of this freedom? According to "God" in Neale Donald Walsch's *Friendship with God*, we are constantly creating ourselves anew. "Many people do not understand this. They do not understand that this is what is happening, that this is what they are doing. They do not know that this is, in fact, *the purpose of all life.* Because they do not know this, they do not realize how important, how impactful, every decision is. Every decision you make—*every* decision—is not a decision about what to do. It's a decision about Who You *Are.* When you see this, when you understand it, everything changes. You begin to see life in a new way. All events, occurrences, and situations turn into opportunities to do what you came here to do ... to announce and to declare, to be and to express, to experience and to fulfill Who You Really Are."

Angels see through the illusion—these Halloween costumes of body and ego—to Who We Really Are. They know our true potential and want to help us reach it.

The least you need to know about freedom: you are a creative being. Your choices determine who you are, and your angels, guardians, and guides will never make decisions for you. They will offer suggestions, but they will always respect your freedom, even when your choices become "mistakes." During the difficult times, they will stay by your side, cushion your fall, and help you understand why a particular growth lesson occurred.

Enhancer 3: Nonlinear Time

David Bohm, the brilliant quantum physicist whom Albert Einstein considered his successor, asserted that the universe was an enormous, magnificently detailed hologram. Thanks to a number of experiments—many of which proved Quantum Entanglement, the so-called "God Effect" that demonstrates a synchronicity of events and split-second (faster than the speed of light) communication between particles, no matter how great the "distance" between them—and support by eminent scientists like neurophysiologist Karl Pribram and physicist F. David Peat, Bohm's theory has gained wide acceptance.

The holographic model of the universe turns our basic understanding/daily illusion of time, space, and matter on its head. It also explains universal laws like the Law of Attraction and a plethora of "supernatural" phenomena, like telepathy and the psychic senses (to be discussed in the next chapter). And it's not just theory; Quantum Entanglement is already being used in encryption, quantum computing, and quantum teleportation.

Let's put our perception and use of timelines on the back burner for a moment so we can discuss what's really going on. In our holographic universe, time is nonlinear, which means that it doesn't move in one direction at a regular rate. Instead, it's simultaneous: the past, present, and future merge into "the eternal now." As a result, our spirits "stretch" to encompass and experience a number of simultaneous lives. That's why emotions and memories from other lifetimes can bleed into our current ones and why guides, guardians, and other spirits linked to those lives—"past" and "future"—show up in our present reality.

It's also why the advice of our angels and guides is so important. They work outside of time-bound awareness. They can see the consequence of every choice we could ever make because all of it—every potential—exists *right now,* and they're not distracted by linear illusions.

Neal Donald Walsch's *Friendship with God* describes the framework as similar to a giant CD-ROM. "Every possible outcome has already been 'programmed.' We experience the outcome we produce by the choices we make— like playing games with a computer. All of the computer's moves already exist. Which outcome you experience depends on which move *you* make." The akashic records are constantly updated, depending on the choices we make with our free will.

The angels are fully aware of this construct and can easily access every preprogrammed potential. Because they see all time as now, they know exactly how each of our choices will affect those concerned and, ultimately, the entire universe.

The least you need to know about nonlinear time: The past and the future are illusions; everything is happening NOW. Seen in a linear light, you chose many aspects of your life before you were ever born, but you never stop cocreating your destiny through thoughts, words, and deeds. Right this moment, everything you ever wanted to be or ever will be is possible because IT'S ALL HAPPENING NOW. Angels—who function within that awareness of the eternal now—know every detail of your potential creations, so their advice is sound and will ultimately lead you to fulfill the destiny your eternal soul is choosing.

Enhancer 4: Nonlocality of the Spirit

We all know our choices affect everyone immediately concerned with them, but you might be wondering why or how "li'l ol' you" could affect the whole universe. A perfect example of the concept can be found in a quote from the 1981 movie *Excalibur,* which some of you may remember. The character Merlin says, "When a man lies, he murders some part of the world."

This idea isn't new; it's ancient wisdom that fits perfectly with the holographic nature of reality—in which everything is one—and helps us understand that the spirit is limitless and without spatial restrictions, in other words, *nonlocal.* Deepak Chopra explains, "Imagine the ocean as nonlocal reality, the field of infinite possibilities, the virtual level of existence that synchronizes everything. Each of us is like a wave in that ocean. We are created from it, and it makes up the very core of who we are. Just as a wave takes on a specific shape, we, too, take on intricate patterns of nonlocal reality."

Whatever the wave's shape and size, it's still made of ocean water. Regardless of a spirit's "shape" or identity, it retains its nonlocal (unrestricted) core. It can be in more than one place at a time ... in fact, in as many places as it wants to be.

Look at holograms. Each individual part contains all of the information of the whole; in essence, every part is the whole. From this perspective, when you attract or tap into something "else"—an animal, a romantic mate, an angel—you're attracting or tapping into something that's already part of you. When you help or hurt another, you help or hurt not only yourself but the whole. Our inherent knowledge of this inseparable union, along with frequent reminders by angels and guides, inspired many ancient cultures and nearly every documented religion with the Golden Rule—to do unto others as we would have them do to us—and variants of it: for example, Jesus's instruction that "whatsoever you do to the least of my brothers, that you do unto me."

Ralph Waldo Emerson's perception of the one, great hologram—although he didn't use that word—appeared in his 1841 essay, "The Oversoul." He described it as "that great nature in which we rest, as the earth lies in the soft arms of the atmosphere; that Unity, that Oversoul, within which every man's particular being is contained and made one with all other; that common heart."

He went on to say, "We live in succession, in division, in parts, in particles. Meantime within man is the soul of the whole; the wise silence; the universal beauty, to which every part and particle is equally related, the eternal ONE. And this deep power in which we exist and whose beatitude is all accessible to us, is not only self-sufficient and perfect in every hour, but the act of seeing and the thing seen, the seer and the spectacle, the subject and the object, are one. We see the world piece by piece, the sun, the moon, the animal, the tree; but the whole, of which these are shining parts, is the soul."

This oversoul or grand hologram—of which you are a part—is everywhere at once (nonlocal). So is the real you, your spirit. And guess what? *Your consciousness can go along for the ride.*

Descriptions of out-of-body experiences and astral travel are plentiful, and those brave enough to acknowledge such events agree that a spirit can travel any distance in the blink of an eye. You need only think of a person, place, or thing, and poof!—it's there, or you yourself are there in spirit. Our bodies might be "local," but our spirits are not.

It's all a bit mind-boggling, I know. But our spirits really do keep a lot of plates spinning at the same time, and sometimes we can catch them in the act!

I'm talking about bilocation, although "bi" indicates two, and spirits can actually be in an infinite number of places all at once. Even a makeshift word like "millilocation" would be insufficient, so let's just stick with the "bi" form.

Bilocation—a phenomenon observed by quantum physicists and everyday people alike—is part and parcel of the spirit world. It doesn't just happen when we're meditating or asleep, or even when our conscious minds are aware of it. I've repeatedly witnessed this phenomenon firsthand or via others, and history is peppered with so-called doppelgangers: for Elizabeth I, Sister Mary of Jesus, Percy Bysse Shelley, and Sir Frederic Carne Rasch, to name only a handful.

Just like our true selves (spirits), angels, guardians, and guides can be everywhere at once, in an instant. Knowing this fact is crucial to working with them. Why? Because many people worry about bothering archangels, ascended masters, and even spirit guides with their "trivial" troubles. Some don't even feel worthy of spiritual support.

At the other end of the spectrum are people who believe they're so "righteous" that they hold a monopoly on the attentions and help of specific spirits. That's just not so! True, a person who focuses the bulk of his/her energy on a specific angel or spirit will get to know that being quite well and can count on their assistance and/or compassion in a bad situation. However, love and acknowledgement aren't reserved for a select "chosen" few. The door is open to all.

Call and you will be heard. Seek and ye shall find.

Angels and other spirits aren't limited by time, place, or something so negligible as number. So the next time you feel alone or too insignificant to attract the notice of archangels, think again. When you imagine you're bothering an angel or other benevolent being with your company, relax. They can be with as many people as request their presence.

We're all spirit, and all of spirit is connected. When you tug at the spirit world—even through thought—it responds. When we call on our angels, guardians, and guides, they feel the pull because we're all one and innately capable of being anywhere and any*when* our spirits need to be.

In an instant.

All at the same time.

The least you need to know about nonlocality: angels can be with everyone and everything that has ever existed or ever will exist *all at once,* because spirit is nonlocal. Call on them whenever you choose. They will always hear you and can fly to your side fast as lightning.

So, to recap, there are four **essentials** to connecting with angels:

- a belief in them;
- the realization that they're everywhere;
- a willingness to connect and communicate; and
- remembrance that you yourself are a spirit.

In addition, there are four **enhancers** that amp up that connection:

- unconditional love;
- freedom;
- nonlinear time; and
- nonlocality of the spirit.

5

How to Communicate with Angels

You don't have to be a professional psychic to communicate with angels. Anyone can do it, because every one of us was born with psychic ability. Think of it as your spiritual birthright. It may be buried so deep an excavation is required, but it's always there, waiting to be tapped.

In Neale Donald Walsch's *Conversations with God* (Book 3), "God" says, "Psychic power is simply the ability to step out of your limited experience into a broader view. To step back. To feel more than what the limited individual you have imagined yourself to be would feel; to know more than he or she would know. It is the ability to tap into the *larger truth* all around you; to sense a different energy."

That psychic power reveals itself in a variety of ways, chiefly through the psychic senses known as "the four clairs":

1. **clairvoyance (clear seeing)**—the ability to see things not visible to the naked eye or which come from another dimension: auras, chakras (energy centers of the human body), occurrences or health-related issues inside the body, objects or events from the past, future events, and ghosts, angels, or other inhabitants of the spirit world seen through dreams, physical eyesight, and visions—either static images or a running "movie"—in the mind's eye

2. **clairaudience (clear hearing)**—the ability to hear music, voices—which can sound like one's own voice or someone else's—or other sounds that originate in another dimension

3. **clairsentience (clear feeling)**—the ability to experience thoughts, messages, emotions or physical feelings—especially someone else's—as an emotional or bodily sensation; includes gut feelings, intuition, and physical sensations such as changes in temperature or air pressure, tingling, chill bumps—even in sauna-like temperatures—or downright touches

from invisible guests, all of which make you
a human barometer for paranormal activity

4. **claircognizance (clear/inner knowing)** —
the ability to receive information, ideas, or
an overwhelming, all-encompassing sense of
knowing "out of the blue," often downloaded
from the akashic records; claircognizants simply
know, even if they're not sure how they know.

Angels—actually, all spirits—can use the four clairs
to communicate with us. And remember, *we* are spirits
too, so we can connect to each other through our
psychic senses. We don't always get the "memo." Other
times, we do repeatedly but choose to ignore it. Undaunted, our ethereal aids continue to send messages,
perhaps because they themselves are messages.

A word to the wise: angels and guides may give
strong messages, but they're always positive and loving.
If you hear or feel any message that's fear-based, critical,
judgmental, abusive, competitive, or destructive, either
a dark entity or most often your own ego is the source.

How Angels Contact Us

Benevolent spirits—angelic or not—contact even the
most dogged skeptics through dreams, number sequences, the three "S"s (symbols, signs, and synchronicity), children, and repetition. People often write off
these experiences as fitful dreams, coincidence, or
overactive imagination, but—like it or not—they occur.

Dreams

Dreams are perfect opportunities for angels to catch us when our guard is down and make their presence known. If you have trouble remembering your dreams, keep a pen and paper near your bed; that way, the moment you wake, you can scribble down your impressions. If you're gung ho on deciphering the dreamscape—or start to notice your primary contact with angels comes during dreams—keep a dream journal. When you have lucid dreams, during which you realize you're dreaming while still in the dream state, make the most of it: invite specific angels to join you; ask them as many questions as you can think of; and concentrate on memorizing the details. You'll be surprised by how much information you glean from this practice.

You can learn the angels' names, details of "past" lives—yours as well as others'—and even hints about future events. In fact, that's how I discovered I was pregnant, via Archangel Metatron, the very night I conceived!

In my experience, the angels don't move their mouths but communicate telepathically. Sylvia Browne's experience concurs. In *Phenomenon*, she states that angels never speak but use telepathic communication instead. However, their telepathy is so strong and effective that humans often believe words are spoken.

Though awesome by nature, angels always leave me with a sense of comfort and support. I'll never forget a dream I had shortly after my family moved into our current home. I welcomed four exceptionally tall visitors into the house. Donned in royal blue robes, they appeared more male than female, but I couldn't definitively conclude their sex. Their facial features were beautifully chiseled... so perfect, in fact, that they might've been wearing makeup. Their skin seemed to glitter, rather like a toned-down version of the dancing-diamonds effect on the sunlit *Twilight* vampires. They emanated power and inspired reverence. Not a word was spoken, but I sensed they were there to help.

The first to enter had straight, shoulder-length, blond hair and sapphire eyes that bored into mine. Of three things I was certain: 1. he/she/it was not and had never been human; 2. it was connected to me in some way; and 3. it knew a lot more about me than I did myself.

Several weeks later, I consulted a professional psychic about other matters. Without any knowledge of my dream, she seemed to validate it.

"You have a very protected house," she said. "I'm seeing a blue angel in the Order of Michael who's keeping you safe. There's also one for your husband and one for each of your boys. These are extremely powerful angels. An entire family only needs one, and your house has four! It has to do with who you are and who you're becoming."

An ominous statement if ever I heard one! I wasn't going to touch it with a ten-foot pole! It would've been nice, though, if those angels had given me a clue in my dream. Perhaps they did, and their tidings are tucked away in my subconscious.

After a lifetime of such dream encounters, I can usually discern whether I've encountered angels or spirit guides, something we'll cover in chapter 9. If they're incredibly tall, luminous, or beautiful beyond belief, typically in an androgynous way, they're angels. If they look human but make direct eye contact, they're guides. That's how they appear to me, anyway. Your experience might be quite different.

Number Sequences

The universe is magical and mysterious, but it's also mathematical. Even music can be translated into mathematical equations. Pythagoras, Plato, and Ptolemy believed in the numerical proportions and musical harmony of the Sun, Moon, and planets. In the seventeenth century, Johannes Kepler blended math, astronomy, and astrology into what he termed "celestial physics." The whole study of numerology is based on the mystical, energetic relationship between numbers and all of life. It only stands to reason that angels would use everything at their—and our—disposal to communicate with us.

A decade ago, I first heard the view that angels speak to us through number sequences. Apparently, angels draw our attention to repetitive numbers: numbers with the same, repeated digit as in 111 or 222; a specific number in more than one place simultaneously, as when you see the number 348 on the license plates of two cars right in front of you; or the same number several places within a short period of time when, for instance, you see $34.57 on a restaurant bill, 3457 written in chalk on the sidewalk, then 3457 as a house number you notice by glancing up at just the right moment, all within 48 hours.

Since that time, I've seen 11:11 on clocks so often it's ridiculous. 933 and 944 also figure largely in my life. One night, I even woke up at 1:11, 2:22, 3:33, 4:44, and 5:55. How's that for crazy?

At any rate, there are a variety of sources on "angel numbers," but Doreen Virtue wrote the definitive work, *Angel Numbers 101: the Meaning of 111, 123, 444, and Other Number Sequences*. She maintains that angels taught her the vibrational meanings of specific numbers and groups of numbers. Here are a few basic correlations:

0: a message from/about God

1: the power of thought in manifestation

2: faith and trust

3: a message from/about ascended masters or energies identified as gods and goddesses

4: a message from angels and/or archangels

5: change

6: physical and material concerns

7: opportunities and angelic encouragement

8: abundance in general, finances in particular

9: your "divine life purpose," or a spiritually based career, passion, or mission you've chosen to fulfill

An individual number combined with others produces a meaning that draws on the energy of all of the digits. For example, Virtue gives the meaning of 348 as "The angels and ascended masters are helping you tap into the universal flow of abundance. Open your arms and receive!"

If you notice a pattern in your life that has anything to do with numbers and want specific messages, I suggest you consult Virtue's book. As you read the various meanings of number sequences, the angels will tell you through visions, thoughts, and/or intuition how the message applies to your situation.

When combined with other forms of angelic communication, number sequences can help us flesh out messages. Here's an example of such a combination.

A year ago, during a family road trip, our car was stopped at a red light. Directly in front of us was a semi-trailer truck with the word "RAVEN" emblazoned across its back.

It wasn't the first time a "RAVEN" truck crossed my path—and ravens, as symbols and actual birds, have come to me for years—but the license plate also included the numbers 444. I shifted my gaze from the license to the clock on our dashboard. It read 4:44 p.m. Then I noticed a billboard to my right; it also contained the number sequence 444.

Angel Numbers 101 records the following message for 444. "There are angels—they're everywhere around you! You are completely loved, supported, and guided by many Heavenly beings, and you have nothing to fear."

Nice message, but it was tied to ravens. What do they symbolize?

In *Animal-Speak: The Spiritual and Magical Powers of Creatures Great and Small*, Ted Andrews explains, "In Scandinavian lore, the raven played a significant role. The Norse god Odin had a pair of ravens who were his messengers. Their names were Hugin (thought) and Munin (memory). Odin was known to shapeshift as a raven himself.

"Each of us has a magician within, and it is Raven which can show us how to bring that part of us out of the dark into the light. Raven speaks of messages from the spirit realm that can shapeshift your life dramatically."

The raven was a symbol specific to my situation. It signified a message from the spirit realm, and the number sequence 444 identified the messengers as angels. Furthermore, the raven symbol was linked to the Norse god Odin—the cornerstone of spiritual beliefs I held in a past life I was exploring at the time—and associated with Archangels Azrael, Cassiel, and Raziel, who I believe helped me to unearth information about that life. As you can see, cross-referencing sources—e.g., *Angel Numbers 101* and *Animal-Speak*—can help you decipher the messages that are coming your way.

We'll discuss the rule of three under "Repetition." For now, take note of the following: the number sequence had three 4s; I saw it in three places at once; and three archangels assisted me.

Symbols, Signs, and Synchronicity
Symbols
The raven symbol in the previous story is just one example. Symbols are representations, oftentimes of specific entities (people, angels, businesses, etc.) or concepts,

which can appear in any form. Then it's up to us to detect the meaning.

Let's say you're petrified of death, and you start to notice the frequency with which you come across—or your mind clairvoyantly generates—a particular image: the ankh, or "handled cross." It would be a good idea to take a few minutes out of your busy day to research that symbol, either on the Internet or at the library. While doing the research, you should pay attention to your inner monologue or any hunches you receive.

As the Egyptian hieroglyph for eternal life, the ankh might be a soothing, angelic reminder that death is an illusion and you have nothing to fear. It could also symbolize a past life in ancient Egypt you're meant to uncover. Acceptance of that lifetime—and the idea of reincarnation—would help you view death as a transition, not an end.

Signs

Let's extend the example with signs. Signs are objects or occurrences which point the way toward something else, like specific information, the source of that information, or a choice/direction along your path.

So you notice that the ankh symbol is appearing everywhere, even in your dreams. Next, you pick up a magazine in a waiting room, and the first page you turn to has a reference to ancient Egypt. Even as your brain registers that fact, the song "(Don't Fear) The Reaper" blasts from a passing car outside. These signs would lead me to suspect that the Archangel Azrael, a.k.a. the

Angel of Death, is responsible for the recurring ankh symbol and is helping you open up to all it represents.

But how do you know if a symbol or sign is a message from Spirit?

Listen to your intuition. In *Praying with Angels*, Richard Webster declares that most intuitive sparks are angelic messages. Sylvia Browne, in *Phenomenon*, credits spirit guides instead. I believe it's a combination of both—direct communication from angels *and* spirit guides—plus something extra: that core part inside each of us which is one with God. The part that's not subject to linear, time-bound awareness. The part that views things from a cosmic, contextual perspective and takes every factor into account.

"God" in Neale Donald Walsch's *Conversations with God* (Book 3) advises, "Pay attention to every hunch you have, every feeling you feel, every intuitive 'hit' you experience. *Pay attention.* Then, act on what you know. Don't let your mind talk you out of it. Don't let your fear pull you away from it. The more that you act on your intuition fearlessly, the more your intuition will serve you. It was always there, only now you're paying attention to it."

Just ask. If you still have doubt, ask the angels—out loud, in your mind, or even on paper—and wait for a response, which will sound like an inner voice giving you an answer. Start with straightforward questions that will prompt a "yes" or "no" first. For example, "Did you put that feather in my path?" Once you're used to receiving answers of the yes/no variety, you can move on to more complex questions.

If you're just looking for yes/no answers, you might receive them through sensation instead of words, especially if you lean toward clairsentience. Start by saying—out loud or in your mind—a true statement, such as, "I love chocolate." Notice any signals your body gives you: for example, a pervading sense of peace or a tingling sensation in one hand. Then say a false statement, such as, "I hate chocolate." Again, notice your body's reaction. Does your stomach churn? Do you feel a tingling sensation in your other hand? Once you know your body's signals, you can use them to discern true from false, yes from no. Dowsing rods and pendulums serve the same purpose, but if you learn to trust your body, you can receive answers anytime, anywhere, and no one but you need know about it.

Synchronicity

Synchronicity is "coincidence," i.e., many incidents happening at or around the same time or place which seems related. When it happens, it's pretty hard to miss.

Signs and synchronicity often work together, as they did toward the end of my Year from Hell. I was working part-time at a used bookstore, which mercifully gave me a focus other than my tortured body. Still, I prayed for relief, and it wasn't long before my thoughts veered toward a key event from my past: the time my father and I received spontaneous healings at

St. David's Cathedral in Wales. I started to wonder if such a thing could happen twice. When I mentioned the idea to my husband, Dan, he was all for a trip to Wales; his only concern was the cost.

The next day, a customer I'd never met strolled into the bookstore with the clear intention of chatting. She expressed her love of travel, and I mentioned my desire to revisit Wales.

She lit up and revealed that she'd be in Wales the following month. Her daughter lived in Pembroke and was getting married in, of all places, St. David's Cathedral.

Was it a sign? My gut told me it was, but I doubted myself.

That night, when Dan picked me up from work, he chose a different route home. A few miles down the road, a giant sign loomed to our right. It contained a single word written in all caps: WALES. Yes, signs can be literal signs!

The hair on the back of my neck stood on end. Even Dan was lost for words.

Once we arrived home, we sat down and pored over our finances, squeezing what money we could from an already compressed budget. Next, I called several airlines to determine a likely fare and perused a book on British bed & breakfasts I'd bought on a whim—or an angelic whisper—a few months earlier. When all was said and done, we were $600 short for a trip to Wales.

Two days later, as we arrived home from shopping, I noticed two young men outside the neighboring apartment. They were definitely Asian, and they were speaking what sounded like Thai. I'd seen them once before, on a day when the air was soft with snowflakes.

Now one of them glanced at me, and I smiled. We exchanged a few pleasantries, and I learned he was indeed from Thailand. Then I started for the stairs.

Not five minutes later, the Thai guy knocked on our apartment door and, quite unexpectedly, asked if I would teach him English.

"Actually, I used to teach English," I replied, "but that was a long time ago."

"I go home soon," he said. "Maybe one month. Not much time. I have money to pay you. Is $600 enough?"

I was flabbergasted. It was the exact amount we needed. Had he pulled that number out of a hat? Or had an angel whispered in his ear?

He assured me that he didn't need the money. When he returned home, he was going to become a monk.

How could I refuse? Signs and synchronicity pointed with precision toward a trip to Wales.

If you open yourself up to the limitless possibilities of the holographic, interconnected universe, you'll see a world of wonder and guidance. When the symbols, signs, and synchronicity show up, your heightened awareness will detect them, and with the help of the spirits who sent them, you'll understand.

Children

I firmly believe that all children are psychic, a view increasingly shared by many psychics, including Sylvia Browne, who wrote about her findings in *Psychic Children: Revealing the Intuitive Gifts and Hidden Abilities of Boys and Girls.* If the word "psychic" disturbs you, think of it as a natural ability to maintain a heightened state of awareness. It might seem extraordinary, but it's really just par for the course. It's adults who are "gifted" enough to create the illusions of separateness, solidity, and stagnation.

Children tap into the true, limitless nature of the universe because they're still as attuned to the unseen—the world of Spirit and womb of creation from which they've just sprung—as they are to the seen, i.e., the material world they've entered. Perhaps the biggest mistake parents make is assuming that their children's perceptions are just imagination, especially when those perceptions deviate from the parents' own ideas. In fact, many imaginary friends are really angels or spirit guides, who can appear as either a child or an adult.

Imagination plays a role, to be sure. But parents who spend any quality time with their children—and who keep an open mind—can usually sense whether their kids' assertions are rooted in fact or fancy. If you really think about it, most of you parents *know* whether your child is truly scared or just faking to escape bedtime. And if you have more than one child, they often corroborate each other's stories.

The next time your child claims to see something you don't, listen to your gut. Notice your reaction to the information. Do chill bumps rise on your arms? Does a word or two of confirmation pop into your inner monologue? Have you ever felt followed or uneasy in the same hallway to which your child is pointing? Pay attention to these clues, as they can reveal the truth of the matter.

When you're attuned to the spirit world, as children are, fear of the dark may stem from the fact that ghosts and spirits are easier to see in dim or dark environments. Fear of the unknown might cause them to mistake an angel or guide for a bogeyman. Nightlights are helpful, and a handy flashlight can empower children to feel more comfortable with the added dimensions they're seeing.

In *Your Psychic Child: How to Raise Intuitive and Spiritually Gifted Kids of All Ages,* Sara Wiseman discusses the "psychic opening" (the expansion of awareness) in adults. But children, she stresses, are open right from the beginning.

When considering the labels placed on many of today's children—e.g., Indigo, Crystal, Star, and Rainbow—Wiseman writes, "For reasons beyond our understanding, today's kids are more psychic than they've ever been ... In a nutshell, it's because they've evolved to be that way."

Each new generation builds on the previous one, honing skills and tapping into innate abilities their parents and grandparents either ignored or never dreamed existed. What past generations used only in part, today's children access with ease.

For an in-depth look at the subject, Browne's *Psychic Children* and Wiseman's *Your Psychic Child* are great resources. In the meantime, do yourself a favor and really listen to the little tykes around you. You'll get an earful!

A friend of mine heard her six-year-old son talking with an "invisible friend" on several occasions. Then one day, the child stopped in the middle of the stairs and refused to proceed downward. When his mother questioned him, he said, "I can't go down yet. He's too big, and he's blocking my way." She asked who "he" was, and the boy said, "Michael, the angel."

When my own boys were six, they made some interesting comments one night as my husband and I tucked them in bed.

"Mommy," Connor said, "what's that purple light behind you?"

I was standing in front of their window, so I turned and observed nothing but the closed blinds. "I don't see anything, honey," I said. "Maybe you saw a car light or my shadow."

He shook his head. "It wasn't a car, and it's not a shadow. It's a big bird creature with round wings."

"Well, whatever it is, it's not bad," I said. "I don't feel anything but good around me."

A minute later, Geoffrey said, "I think it was one of your angels, Mommy."

"Why?" I asked. "Because it was behind me?"

"No," he replied. "Because it was purple."

Apparently, the boys spotted purple angels all over our house, but mostly around me. A sudden and surprising correlation struck me: for my entire life, the predominant color I saw in the dark or behind closed eyes was purple.

Don't sell kids short. Their unbiased perceptions can strengthen and expand your own spiritual awareness.

Repetition

Broken records—back when people actually listened to records—drew attention by repeating the same bit of music over and over again. Angels often deliver messages in the same way. It's a little like synchronicity, but repetition deals with specific, often word-for-word messages.

Repeatedly seeing a bumper sticker might be common enough. But when that bumper sticker matches verbatim something you believe the angels told you the night before, you're on to something. The same line of poetry quoted to you by three different people in the same day is also a tip-off. Song lyrics, the written word, or random comments by friends and strangers alike: all can be conduits for divine messages, and they get the job done through repetition.

Let's talk music. Barely four hours after my vision of the fiery, blue eye (see the info on Archangel Michael in chapter 3), I flicked on the car radio. The first song I heard was the Guns N' Roses tune "Patience." Obviously, the title was right in line with the counsel

I received during my astral trip. It was one message I grasped with only one reprise.

Other messages take some time to sink in. In recent years, two particular songs have featured in my life, whether I was at the grocery store, in my chiropractor's waiting room, in elevators, or surfing TV channels. Whenever I grew weary of the uphill battle to get published, I heard Olivia Newton-John's 1980 hit, "Magic." Even now, when I doubt myself during the writing process, I hear "Sing," the song written for *Sesame Street* and popularized by The Carpenters's 1973 release.

Don't forget, angels can plant any kind of image or thought into your head, as well as everyone else's. That song you can't stop humming might contain a message.

If you're stubborn, messages will repeat themselves as many times as need be. If you get the hint, once is all it takes. However, some folks rely on the rule of three; they regard a message as valid only after it appears three times.

Three is the smallest number of elements necessary to produce a pattern, and the number "three" has long been associated with magic and mysticism. Perhaps this is true because most of us perceive ourselves living within a three-dimensional construct. Furthermore, people tend to process and recall information better when it's introduced in threes.

Trios appear in both expert and everyday knowledge. Music, math, comedy, religion, business, economics, fairytales, and famous speeches all invoke the power of three. You may recognize the following examples:

"Friends, Romans, countrymen"; "life, liberty, and the pursuit of happiness"; "government of the people, by the people, and for the people"; "Location, location, location"; "Stop, look, and listen"; the Three Little Pigs; the Three Little Kittens; Goldilocks and the Three Bears; the so-called "triple threat"; triad chords in music; body, mind, spirit; the Wiccan Law of Threefold Return; three Magi presenting three gifts to the infant Jesus. And long before the Christian trinity was envisioned, holy trinities/triple deities emerged in various cultures around the world.

The rule of three isn't an angelic rule; once is enough when the recipient is aware and open to advice. Still, it can help those who doubt their powers of perception, or those who trust rules and patterns over instinct. That said, please don't let this rule dominate or restrict the flow of your communication with angels.

The important thing is to listen up! Messages are everywhere, just like the messengers who carry them. Dreams, number sequences, the three "S"s, children, and repetition are all channels for angelic communication.

How We Initiate Contact

All you have to do is think about angels, and you attract them. You can also ask God to send you angels or call them directly. You can talk to them out loud or in your mind.

You can think, *Angels, please help me!* and they'll be with you instantly. I've experienced this truth so many times that now, I just trust it.

Visualization is another technique for calling angels to your side. In *Angel Therapy: Healing Messages for Every Area of Your Life*, Doreen Virtue elaborates: "See the angels flying in circles around you or loved ones. See powerful angels thronged by your side. See the room you are in crowded with thousands of angels. These visualizations are angelic invocations that create your reality."

Remember, when you talk to the angels, do so openly and freely. Psychic Medium and Certified Angel Therapy Practitioner Angela Hartfield says that angels prefer to be treated like family. Likewise, Chantel Lysette refers to angels as our brothers and sisters.

How would you ask a trusted brother or sister for help? Ask angels for help in the same way. The difference is that angels, unlike family members, can be anywhere they need to be in an instant and coordinate their efforts with other angels and spirits who are involved. For a list of specific needs, along with archangels who specialize in them, see the appendix. In the meantime, here are a couple of examples:

1. You're worried about an issue your daughter is facing at school, so you call on Archangel Metatron. "Metatron, I know you can help (insert child's name). Please be with her as she goes about her day. Give her a sense of peace and security in this situation, and encourage everyone concerned to act from their highest selves. Thank you."

2. You're furious about something and don't want
   to take it out on your family. Call on Archangel
   Michael and tell it like it is. "Okay, Michael,
   I really need your help. I'm so mad I can't even
   see straight, but I don't want to upset everyone
   else. Please help me get rid of this negativity and
   replace it with good energy ASAP. Thank you."

You can't fool angels, so you might as well be frank
with them. As with all relationships, sincerity breeds
success. And whether or not you attach "archangel" to
the name—for instance, "Archangel Michael" or just
plain "Michael"—the relevant angel knows instinctively
who you're expecting. Thought and feeling are at the
core of angelic communication, not language.

At first, you may be drawn toward one of the many
angel card decks on the market. Such cards can definitely
familiarize you with the angelic realm, and in some cases,
build your confidence and increase your comfort level.
However, as Lysette points out in *The Angel Code*, they can
become a crutch. The power to communicate with angels
is *inside you.*

You are the conduit for information. You interpret
the messages.

Two techniques open the floodgates to full-blown
communication. They are channeling and meditation.

Channeling

Don't let that word scare you. You're already a channel for circulating, universal energy—what Deepak Chopra calls the "quantum soup"—just by *being*. Now it's time to consider tuning in to angelic messages.

One form of channeling, suggested by authors such as Doreen Virtue and Richard Webster, is automatic writing. It's considered automatic because there's no conscious effort or thought involved. You simply invite an angel or angels into your space and ask them to communicate through you via whatever instrument you choose, whether a pen or a computer keyboard. Then you either "zone out" or focus on something else, for example, a television show. The angel(s) take control of the instrument, and you allow it to move freely. With practice, your doodles—or typed gibberish—become words and phrases, many of which are angelic messages.

If that method of channeling appeals to you, give it a try. However, most beginners will find another method far easier. Webster calls it "automatic dictation," and it involves asking the angels for advice and consciously writing down the answers that come to you. If you're working with a friend or spouse, he/she asks the questions aloud and writes down—or types—your responses, and vice versa.

Channel/Psychic Medium Kim O'Neill simply refers to this technique as "channeling." She believes that angels and guides are responsible for as much as 80 to 85 percent of the information flowing through our brains, and in her audio CD, *Communicating with Your Angels*, she gives easy directions for accessing it.

In her view, the more complicated the process, the less likely people are to attempt it. I'm all too familiar with the hectic pace of modern life and the potential chaos kids add to the mix, so I completely agree. I'll add only two steps to O'Neill's method, and they will appear in italics.

1. Set aside a 30- to 45-minute block of time at least once a week for channeling.

2. Prepare a list of questions you'd like answered.

3. At the appointed time, go to a quiet place, even if it's just inside your parked car.

4. Close your eyes. Take a deep breath, then let it out completely.

5. *Imagine white light pouring down on you from above so that it fills you and encases you in a bubble of divine love and protection. Then ask your angels, guardians, and guides—either in general or using specific names—to join you and help you receive the most accurate information possible.*

6. Say aloud, "Brain, shut off."

7. Speak your first question out loud and listen for an answer. It will appear, usually within 5 to 10 seconds, as thoughts in your mind or an actual voice. Record any response you "hear." Continue with your other questions,

posing them in your mind or out loud.
Toward the end of the session, give
the angels an open floor, i.e., a chance
to tell you whatever they want you to know.

8. *Thank the angels or whomever you contacted for the
information you received.*

And that's it. At first, you might feel like you're talking to yourself, or that some of the responses are merely
wishful thinking. If you're unsure whether the answers
are coming from you or the angels, ask them about it.
You can also experiment with channeling at different
times during the day to determine when you "hear" the
best. Everyone's different: while one person might channel better at night, another will prefer the crack of dawn.
In the beginning, you might pick up only concise replies
like "yes," "no," "soon," "seven weeks," or "brown." But
soon, the answers will flesh out with details that will surprise you and your channeling partner, if you have one.

The more you channel, the greater confidence you'll
have in your abilities; when your recorded answers accu-
rately predict something you would never have imagined,
your trust will blossom. You might even slip into automatic writing, or use words and phrases that aren't part
of your known vocabulary, or record names, dates, and
events from history that subsequent research confirms.

For those of you who feel too busy—or too physi-
cally sore, perhaps due to back or joint issues—to sit
for any length of time, you can also walk with angels.

Whether your walk is part of an exercise regimen or just a casual stretch of the legs, you can invite angels to tag along and talk to them in your mind. You probably won't have your list of questions handy, and you won't be able to write any answers down until your walk is over. Nevertheless, your mind will still be the channel for angelic information.

You can also ask the angels—during both channeling and meditation—to validate your communications by sending you a sign. They will then tell you or show you in your mind's eye a specific sign—e.g., blue ribbons, giraffes, a pink balloon, etc.—for which you can be on the lookout. When that particular sign pops up in your experience, you'll know the exchange was real.

By the way, if an angel tells you to watch for a giraffe, it doesn't necessarily mean you'll spot a giraffe browsing in your backyard. But you might see giraffe figurines in a store window or Geoffrey the Giraffe on a Toys "R" Us postcard you receive in the mail. Of course, the more you get to know the angels, the less you'll feel the need for such signs.

Prayers and requests are always answered. However, you may have to exercise a little patience, cultivated largely through trust in the universal intelligence, a.k.a. God. Above all, be patient with *yourself* during the communication process. We're all works in progress, proceeding along our paths just as we should.

Meditation

Meditation can involve emptying the mind, concentration on one specific thing, or visualization, but basically, it allows you to experience your spiritual core. It's a great way to meet angels, guardians, and guides and an opportunity to be calm and creative at once. Imagination—an ability every one of us has—is the key.

In *The Angel Code*, Chantel Lysette describes imagination as a bridge to intuition and the best tool we have for meditation and clairvoyance. "By allowing your imagination to flow, you are engaging in the creative processes of the universe. Because you are moving away from the obstacles of conditioned thought and expectations, you are moving yourself ever closer to direct alignment with the Creator."

Meditation is a personal thing, so people experience it in different ways. If you gravitate toward clairvoyance, visual details will likely be your focal point; you might even see words in front of you as though they were printed on the air. If clairaudience is your thing, you'll hear a variety of sounds and words—eventually whole sentences—that will provide meaning to your experience. Clairsentients often feel their way through the experience; they note the grainy sensation of sand beneath their feet, the warm breeze on their skin, the smooth texture of satin as their hands part curtains before them. Claircognizants might have whole concepts drop into their laps, so to speak. You could experience two, three, or all four of these "clairs" as you meditate.

To communicate with your angels through meditation, I suggest you follow three steps: 1. state your intention for the meditation; 2. perform a quick grounding and cleansing exercise; 3. start the meditation for meeting angels. During the meditation, I'll have you go to a "safe place," a meditative reality that makes you feel free and relaxed, yet gives you a sense of security. Your safe place can be anywhere on earth or beyond: a mountaintop, a beach, a sailboat, a garden, a thatch-roofed cottage, a medieval castle, a temple, a church, a distant planet, etc. The choice is yours. If you love adventure, you can leave that choice up to the particular angel you plan to meet and see where he takes you!

Feel free to tweak the three steps to suit your preferences, but please keep the color sequence (red, orange, yellow, green, blue, indigo, white) the same. The colors represent *in order* the body's chakras, i.e., vortices/centers through which energy is processed.

1. Red: base/root chakra, located at the coccyx; concerns survival and security

2. Orange: sacral chakra, just below the navel; sexuality, creativity

3. Yellow: solar plexus chakra, just above the navel; emotions, personal power

4. Green: heart chakra, center of the chest; love, harmony, compassion

5. Blue: throat chakra, throat; self-expression, communication

6. Indigo or violet: third-eye chakra, centered just above the eyebrows; intuition, clairvoyance

7. White: crown chakra, top of the head; higher consciousness, spiritual link to the divine

The chakra stuff is just for your information, not something you need to memorize. In fact, you don't even have to memorize the meditation; you can simply record yourself reading it and play it back when the time comes, or you can have a friend read it out to you.

As you attempt the meditation, don't worry if you can't visualize a certain object or feel a specific sensation. And don't eject yourself from the experience prematurely because you feel you're "pretending" the whole affair. Remember, imagination is creation in progress. Once you feel comfortable with the process, a natural flow of communication will result.

STEP 1: **State your intention.** For example, you could say aloud, "I intend to meet Archangel Michael in this meditation." Or "I intend to practice clairaudience by meeting several angels."

STEP 2: **Grounding and cleansing.** Stand with your feet apart. Close your eyes and relax. Take a slow, deep breath, and at the same time, imagine the powerful, healing energy of the earth flowing into you through your feet and traveling all the way to the top of your head. It should feel like your inhalation is drawing the earth's energy into you. You can visualize the energy moving upward, hear its deep hum, and/or feel it spreading through your body. Then exhale slowly. Repeat. Inhale again, but this time, as you slowly exhale, imagine a bright white light from above pouring into the top of your head, flowing down through your entire body, washing away all negativity. Repeat.

STEP 3: Time to meditate. Sit in a comfortable position or lie down. Consciously relax your body, beginning with your feet and ending with your head. Listen to the sound of your breathing, then imagine a blanket of peace and love settling over you. Start the meditation.

Meditation for Meeting Angels

Imagine yourself walking along a forest path. Great pillars of birch, maple, and oak surround you. Leaves the color of a brilliant sunset whisper and shake in the gentle breeze. All at once, a shower of red leaves trickles down around you. You pause to revel in the moment and absorb the rich color, then continue on. Soon after, orange leaves rain down on you. Drinking in the vibrant color, you stop again and raise your hands to feel the leaves tickle your palms. Soon, you move onward, only to be met by another downpour: yellow leaves this time. You can't help but smile as a leaf lands on your nose. You brush it off and continue forward.

The bubbling murmur of a stream touches your ears. It's just up ahead, so you proceed toward it. Sunlight dances on the crystalline water. A nearby patch of green grass looks so inviting that you sit down and run your fingers through the soft, emerald blades. You lean back and look up toward a gap in the canopy of trees. You've never seen a sky so blue, and you feel the color's soothing energy seep into your consciousness. You lower your gaze and look to your right, where a wooden bridge spans the stream. Curious, you stand and approach it.

You start to cross the bridge but pause in the middle and place your hands on the wooden railing. Bending slightly, you peer over the side to the water below. The stream is so clear that you can see a number of pebbles and stones beneath the surface. They are every shade of purple you can imagine—from periwinkle to indigo— and you stare at them in wonder, knowing that as you do so, they are opening your inner eye.

Feeling energized and more aware than ever before, you straighten, turn, and cross the bridge to the other side. The growth of trees is thicker here. High above, the interwoven branches resemble the dome of an enormous cathedral. Up ahead, the trees form an archway at the end of a path, and within that arch is a bright white light that hums with the primal energy of the universe. You walk toward it slowly, sensing it's a magical threshold; once you step through that light, you'll enter a dimension where anything is possible. Calm and assured, you step over the threshold, pass through the light, and find yourself in the "safe place" you envisioned.

Explore your safe place. Notice the details, how it looks, sounds, feels, and smells. Imagine yourself doing and experiencing anything you want. Talk to anyone you encounter along the way. Ask who they are and what they'd like to tell you. If they invite you to follow them, go along and be open to whatever they show you. Remember, you're completely safe, and nothing can harm you. You're simply making friends and learning what you can.

When you're ready to leave, picture the archway through which you entered this world. Step through the white light and back into the forest. Cross the bridge, and follow the path out of the woods.

(End of meditation)

Take a few deep breaths and open your eyes. Reflect on your experience and, if you want to keep a record, write down everything you remember about the angels you encountered and their communication with you.

You have nothing to lose and everything to gain from contacting the angels. They've always been around you, helping in ways you may never know. Once you open your heart and mind to them, you'll wonder why you didn't do it sooner!

6

Guardian Angels

The chief difference between guardian angels and other angels is that guardians are with us every moment of every day from the instant we're born until the instant—and possibly after—we arrive at the Other Side. Other angels come and go; a guardian angel sticks to us like glue.

Richard Webster's description in *Praying with Angels* illuminates this point: "Your guardian angel's task is to protect, guide, and look after you throughout this lifetime. He looks after your soul as well as your physical body. Messages from your guardian angel are received as thoughts and intuitions. This is the 'still small voice' that spoke to Elijah on Mount Sinai (1 Kings 19:12) ... At the end of your life, your guardian angel will carry your soul to heaven."

The belief in guardian angels is an ancient one. In his essay, "The Holy Guardian Angel: Exploring the Sacred Magick of Abramelin the Mage," Aaron Leitch observes that shamanic cultures worldwide have this concept of a guardian spirit in common. It may, in fact, be one of the oldest spiritual ideas on Earth.

In the essay, "Angels: a History of Angels in Western Thought," Richard Ebbs highlights the Sumerian belief that each individual had a "ghost" attached to him/her which served as a lifelong companion. Excavations have revealed stone carvings and paintings of winged, human figures on temple walls, as well as altars seemingly dedicated to guardian ghosts in private homes.

The Avesta, the sacred texts of Zoroastrianism, praised guardian spirits called *fravashis* who helped maintain the balance of the universe and watched over individual souls when they entered the material world. During and after the Babylonian captivity, Judaism was greatly influenced by this idea of a personal, angelic representative, yet the term *malakhim* ("messengers") could refer to humans as well as angels. A similar belief of God-sent guardian spirits was common in ancient Greece; in Plato's *Apology of Socrates,* Socrates claimed to have a *daimonion* ("divine something") which verbally warned him against mistakes but never made decisions for him.

The Mesopotamians believed in guardian spirits known as the *šêdu* (the male form) and the *lamassu* (his female counterpart). An ancient incantation was used to summon a good *šêdu* to one's right side and a good *lamassu* to one's left.

The concept of two guardians, one on either side, appeared in Islam as *Kiraman Katibin* ("honorable recorders"), the two angels who write down every thought, feeling, and action a person has throughout his/her life. The angel on one's right shoulder records the good deeds; the one on the left records the bad. *Al-Mu'aqqibat* ("the protectors") keep people from death until its decreed time.

The Christian Bible also supports the idea of spiritual guardians. In Matthew 18:10, Jesus speaks of children's guardian angels: "Take heed that ye despise not one of these little ones; for I say unto you that in heaven their angels do always behold the face of my Father which is in heaven." Three and a half centuries later, St. Jerome declared, "How great the dignity of the soul, since each one has from his birth an angel commissioned to guard it."

In the twentieth century, the founder of Anthroposophy, Rudolf Steiner, took that belief a step further. He maintained that guardian angels stay with us through all of our incarnations. After everything I've seen and learned, I tend to agree with him.

Does everyone have a guardian angel? Does it stay with us every moment from birth to death? Is it a part of our "higher selves"? Is it a separate entity? Though it may seem a contradiction, the answer to all of these questions is YES. I believe we can connect the dots by diving into the rabbit hole of personal experience.

One afternoon, shortly before our children's third birthday, Dan strapped them into their car seats while I waited beside the minivan. Suddenly, Geoffrey's eyes widened at the sight of something outside the car, just behind me.

"Big Geoffrey," he said, pointing.

I turned around but saw nothing.

He pointed. "Big Geoffrey over there."

Naturally, I had to ask, "Who's Big Geoffrey?"

"Big Geoffrey," he repeated, pointing outside. Then he pointed to himself. "Little Geoffrey."

"You're Little Geoffrey?" I asked.

"Yes," he answered.

"Does Big Geoffrey look like you?"

"Different."

"Are you talking about you?" I questioned, wondering if perhaps he saw a vision of his future, older self. On occasion, the boys had seen residual images from the past and what seemed to be visions of the future.

"No," he maintained. "Big Geoffrey."

A sudden inspiration struck me. "Is Big Geoffrey you or an angel?"

"Angel," he affirmed.

Then he smiled, seemingly pleased I understood at last. He dropped the subject, and I was left to suppose we'd been talking about his guardian angel. But why had it hovered at my back? Did it encourage Geoffrey's remarks in order to teach me, perhaps because it knew I would one day write this chapter?

I'd always believed in guardian angels, but I'd never given much thought to their natures. As a little girl, I named one of my first dolls "Angel." With her long blond hair and bangs, Angel seemed like a "little me." Now I wondered if I chose her name because she symbolized a bigger me.

One night about a year after my brush with "Big Geoffrey," I had another odd experience: an angelic infusion of energy, similar to the one I mentioned in chapter 2. I was just crossing the living room to fetch a DVD case when the top of my head began to tingle. It might sound crazy, but my crown felt like it was opening up. All at once, a powerful force poured into it. Soon the sensation spread to my neck, shoulders, arms, and hands. After a minute or two, the "surge" into my head ceased, but my whole body felt lighter, like I could literally float away.

Trust me, I still carry much of the weight I packed on during my twin pregnancy. My figure isn't anyone's idea of "light," but that's the only word that describes the feeling.

I was in my body, yet detached from it. Even so, I felt completely protected and certain that the experience was supposed to happen. Speech seemed superfluous. Sensing and being were all that mattered.

A little while later, I lay in bed in total darkness ... except, that is, for a strange glow which emanated from my body. The sensation of *being* "light" was fading, yet I *looked* like a human nightlight. I couldn't help but wonder if my imagination had done a cannonball into the deepest pool ever constructed, but no—the light was too bright. It had to be real. I lifted the bedcovers off my waist and stared down the length of my legs. Even my feet were luminous.

I slid out of bed, tiptoed from the bedroom, and parked myself in front of the computer. Then I typed my "symptoms" into a search engine and sifted through the resulting data.

One possibility was that I glimpsed the energy of my guardian angel on and around me. Another explanation involved a burgeoning awareness of my "light body."

Apparently, the light body is a person's inner core of light, an etheric grid or matrix contained within the human form which links one's physical, emotional, mental, and spiritual being through a kind of sacred geometry. It's an electromagnetic field of energy and information which radiates from the body and allegedly triggers a specific resonance in each cell, enhancing one's connection to the light of God. Countless others shared my physical symptoms, which were supposed signs of "the ascension process."

Ascension is thought to be the next step in human evolution, a shift from third- to fifth- (or even higher) dimensional consciousness, during which our DNA becomes restranded to hold more light. Others describe it as a merging with one's higher self accomplished by the larger, upper-dimensional part of one's spirit descending into the physical body. Most equate it with spiritual en-lightenment, a complete remembrance of one's unity with the Divine.

The light I'd seen was evidence of both my light body and my guardian angel. That angel—the same being who facilitated my "peak experience" when I was eight—helped me advance along my spiritual path by infusing me with energy from the higher dimensions that height-ened my awareness of both my *inner* core of light and the constant presence of my guardian angel, what some might call an *outer* source of light.

Fast forward to last December when the history and mythology of ancient Egypt wended its way into my research for this book. The ancient Egyptians be-lieved that every person was born with a *ka*, an invis-ible, spiritual double which funneled the creative and supportive life forces from the divine to the individual. The creator-god Khnum (or Khnemu)—known as the "Cosmic Potter" and the "Lord of Created Things from Himself"—was said to mold a man and his *ka* at the same time, and although the *ka* might represent a human soul, it could also guide and guard it. To the an-cient Egyptians, the *ka* was one's link to eternal life.

While reading about this concept, I remembered a passage from Neale Donald Walsch's *Conversations with God* (Book 3) in which "God" identifies the soul's loca-tion. "The soul is *everywhere* in, through, and around you. It is that which contains you ... The soul is *larger than the body*. It is not carried within the body, but carries the body within it ... The soul is that which holds you together—just as *the Soul of God is that which contains the universe, and holds it together.*" So my soul and God's soul—"the same energy, coalesced, compressed in different ways"—were in and around me all the time.

My guardian angel, which was a part of both souls, was basically a constant hug from God. That thought made me feel incredibly protected and—despite my multitude of faults—cherished. Even so, research and rumination weren't enough.

In the end, I asked the angels for a definitive answer to the question most readers would ask: were guardian angels part of us or separate? Word for word, here's the response I received.

The guardian angel is an entity unto itself, created from the soul of the one it serves. Its essence is the love and light of God. So, in a sense, it is both your higher self and a separate entity.

The speed, volume, and clarity of the response astounded me. Even so, I doubted it, but only for a few hours. Confirmation came "out of the mouths of babes" that same day.

Home from school, Connor and Geoffrey played in their bedroom while I typed away at the computer. At one point, Geoffrey stepped into their bathroom. Seconds later, his voice rang out: "Connor! I see an angel!"

"Yeah," his twin replied. "I know."

Connor sounded pretty blasé about the whole thing. I, on the other hand, abandoned the computer to check into it.

"It was right over there," Geoffrey told me, pointing toward the bathtub. "It was purple, so it was one of your angels." Again with the purple angels!

Actually, while sitting at the computer, I *had* wondered what Geoffrey was up to in the bathroom. Had "one of my angels"—or even another aspect of myself—zipped there to find out?

I recalled a "portrait" Geoffrey drew of me in preschool. He colored my entire body (including my head!) and the area around it purple. My first impression upon seeing it was that some kind of purple flame engulfed me. At the time, I speculated that it represented my aura; now I wondered if it signified my guardian angel.

In the present, Geoffrey continued his explanation. "I have an angel like that, too," he said. "They're part of us, but bigger than us and different from us, too. They watch over us and protect us so we won't get hurt, like the angels that saved me when I hit my head on the ground a few years ago. Remember that?"

What are the odds of my son bringing up this subject on the very day I asked the angels about it, while he was still at school? In chapter 5, I mentioned that angels can communicate with us through children. In this instance, they not only conveyed information but confirmed it.

Guardian angels are distinct creations, yet still a part of us, and ultimately, expressions of the one called "God." Everywhere in nature, there are parallels. A single oak tree produces millions of acorns, every one of which contains the essence or blueprint of its source. That blueprint allows an acorn to grow into a form every bit as splendid as the original.

God is the oak, and you are the acorn. Your guardian angel is the intelligence which holds the blueprint, the promise of what you can and *will* become.

Life is an amazing ride, complete with speed bumps of every size. But even before you were born, the essence of your spirit was fashioned into a sacred sentinel who's bound to you 24/7 and dedicated to your soul's journey, however strenuous it might be. So, if you'll excuse the expression, "Buck up, little camper!" Listen to your heart, go out on that limb, and milk every last drop from the life you're creating, secure in the knowledge that your guardian angel is watching over it all ... and loving you every second.

The following is a meditation designed to help you meet your guardian angel. Please see the meditation section in chapter 5 for specific instructions on the three preparatory steps: 1. state your intention for the meditation; 2. perform a quick grounding and cleansing exercise; 3. start the meditation.

To give yourself the greatest chance for success, you should individualize the location. The main thing is that you envision a comfortable room inside of a building that has access to the great outdoors. (This figures into two upcoming meditations: the Meditation for Meeting Guardians and the Meditation for Meeting Spirit Guides.) There should also be two chairs in front of a fireplace. The room might be the "safe place" you created for the Angels meditation. The building can be your own house, your dream home, a country cottage, a castle, etc. It's up to you.

Meditation for Meeting Your Guardian Angel

Imagine yourself walking around your comfortable room. Touch its contents; observe the details. Satisfaction and peace wash over you in this ideal place. Now, sit down in one of the comfortable chairs before the fireplace. The warmth emanating from the hearth relaxes you. The kindling crackles as you stare into the dancing flames.

Suddenly, the fire turns a bright red. The strength and passion of this color inspires you. Gradually, it shifts into a vibrant orange that makes you feel alive and capable of creating anything you desire. After a moment, the blaze becomes a light, buttery yellow that harmonizes your emotions and fills you with confidence and joy. Next, the fire changes to a soothing, healing, emerald green that opens your heart to love and trust. You feel ready and willing to communicate, and the flames respond by displaying dazzling hues of blue. The colors infuse you with a sense of freedom, and then they transform into various shades of purple. Your senses are heightened. Your inner eye opens to allow any vision that will serve you. Finally, the fire reflects all light, appearing white as the purest snow.

As you stare into that white light, you become aware of a presence sitting in the chair beside you. It seems oddly familiar, as though somehow, you've always known it was there. Turn now, and greet your guardian angel.

Notice any details about the angel's appearance. Ask his/her name if you don't already know it and anything else you're curious about. Ask how you can better sense the angel's constant presence. Allow him/her to bring up any relevant subjects. When you're ready for your angel to slip back into invisibility, say good bye and watch it fade from your vision. Return your gaze to the fire, then stand to stretch your limbs. Cast a final glance around your special room and know you can return here whenever you want.

(End of meditation)

Take a few deep breaths and open your eyes. Reflect on your experience, and if you want to keep a record, write down everything you remember about your guardian angel and what you learned.

7

Ascended Masters, the Guardians of Mankind

Supervising the spiritual growth of an entire planet isn't easy, but someone's got to do it! Who better for the task than those enlightened beings known as ascended masters?

They are the great teachers, healers, and prophets who once walked the earth but now guard and guide the evolving human race from the realm of spirit. They sprang from all cultures of the world, and during their earthly lives, they reminded us that we are all sons and daughters of God. Because they reached such high states of spiritual awareness, they served—and still serve—as examples of how to attune ourselves to source energy. Their relationship with God supersedes any religious practice, so they love and respect all seekers of light and their diverse spiritual paths.

The following list of ascended masters is by no means complete, but here are some of the major players:

Babaji

Mahavatar Babaji was a Hindu saint and guru responsible for the revival of Kriya Yoga. He reportedly told his disciple, Lahiri Mahayasa, "The Kriya Yoga which I am giving to the world through you in this 19th century is a revival of the same science which Krishna gave, millenniums ago, to Arjuna, and which was later known to Patanjali, and to Christ, St. John, St. Paul, and other disciples." Between 1861 and 1924, Babaji appeared—always as a young man—in several places near the Himalayas, but many believe he lived for more than 1800 years before sidestepping death and ascending with his physical body. His recorded miracles include levitation, healing the sick, raising the dead, passing through solid matter, manifesting any necessity from thin air, and bilocation, all of which are associated with the known *Siddhis* ("supernatural" abilities largely acquired through the practices of meditation and/or yoga). According to Yogananda's *Autobiography of a Yogi*, published in 1946, Babaji was an *avatara* (a Sanskrit word which indicates Divinity descending into flesh) who communed with another such master, Jesus, and they worked together by emitting the vibrations of peace and redemption to inspire humanity's spiritual evolution. Many believe Babaji was Krishna in a previous life. Krishna was apparently a real historical figure regarded by many as the eighth incarnation of Vishnu, the omniscient, omnipresent, peace-loving deity of the Hindu trinity. Scholars traditionally place his birth between 3200 and 3100 BCE, but a new date—July 21, 3228 BCE—determined through computer astrology is gaining support.

Helps with the following: breathwork (conscious alteration of breathing used for physical, psychological, and/or spiritual benefit, as with yogic and tantric practices), manifestation (creating/attracting what you desire), overcoming addictions, patience, spiritual growth, surrender, yoga

Buddha

Siddharta Gautama was born a prince in Lumbini (in modern Nepal) around 563 BCE, at which time a seer predicted he'd become either a great king or a savior of humanity. As an adult, he became determined to eliminate human suffering, and at age 29, renounced his wealth and royal title to lead an ascetic life. When enlightenment still eluded him, he realized that neither extreme—of self-indulgence or self-denial—held the key. The "Middle Way" (everything in moderation) and meditation created the most harmonious path. At the age of 35, while meditating under a large, sacred fig tree—later known as the Bodhi tree—he achieved enlightenment. As the *Buddha* ("awakened one"), he and his disciples traveled through India's northern plains and taught his spiritual philosophy. Later in life, he established an order of monks and an equivalent order of nuns. Early inscriptional records date from the reign of Asoka (c. 269–232 BCE), but before that, the Buddha's disciples committed his teachings to memory and passed them down through oral tradition. The Buddhist canon, the Tipitaka, was written around 83 BCE and is roughly eleven times the size of the Christian Bible! The Mahayana sutras (scriptural narratives) followed soon after. Although the Buddha discouraged others from following his path merely because they observed miraculous powers, there are accounts of him visiting the spirit world, recalling countless past lives, walking on/levitating above a stream, and parting floodwaters to tread dry land. Perhaps the greatest miracle is the fact that for more than 2,500 years, Buddhism has spread through persuasion, not force. Peace—in this world and in all worlds—is Buddhism's primary goal.

Helps with the following: balance in all things, joy, meditation, peace, spiritual understanding

El Morya

El Morya was first mentioned as an ascended master by Helena Blavatsky, cofounder of the Theosophical Society in the late 1800s. The society advanced the spiritual philosophy known as Theosophy ("god-wisdom" or "divine wisdom"), which sought to unify the beliefs and practices of science, philosophy, and religion, i.e., body, mind, and spirit. El Morya is believed to have incarnated as the son of Enoch, a devotee of Zarathustra, the master mason for the great pyramid, Abraham (the patriarch of Judaism, Christianity, and Islam), Melchior (one of the three *magi,* popularly known as wise men, who traveled to see the infant Jesus), Thomas Becket, Sir Thomas More, and Akbar the Great. His final embodiment was apparently as a nineteenth-century Rajput prince who many claim was Ranbir Singh, the son of Maharaja Gulab Singh. Today, he's considered the Chohan (lord or master) of the First (blue) Ray of God's will. Incidentally, the concept of the Seven Rays—the light emanations from the godhead which "enlighten" humans—didn't start with Theosophy; it appears in Hindu and Christian symbolism, as well as the mythologies of ancient Egypt, Greece, and Rome.

Helps with the following: faith, legal situations, protection, staying grounded

Francis of Assisi, Saint

Born Giovanni Francesco di Bernardone in Assisi, Italy around 1182, Saint Francis became one of the most beloved figures in Christian history. His simple lifestyle, charitable works, deep spirituality, love of nature, preternatural ability to communicate with animals, and universal perspective—which held that all living things were one family and equally important—were like a breath of fresh air. He even viewed God as both mother and father and acknowledged the feminine side of his own personality. On April 16, 1209, Pope Innocent III approved the rule of St. Francis, which eventually included three orders: the Friars Minor, the Poor Ladies or Clares, and the Brothers and Sisters of Penance. In his earthly life and in spirit, he was/is the very thing he sought to be and described in his famous prayer: an instrument of peace. He's reported to have said, "So precious is a person's faith in God, so precious; never should we harm that. Because He gave birth to all religions."

Helps with the following: choosing a meaningful career, communication with animals, environmentalism, healing of animals, recognition and acceptance of one's personal and global responsibilities, remembering one's life purpose, spiritual devotion

Jesus (Yeshua)

The dates of his birth and death are still debated, the former ranging from 8 to 2 BCE; the latter, from 29 to 36 CE. Even the length of his ministry—anywhere from one to three years—is disputed. Regardless, that ministry impacted the world in a big way. Like all great spiritual teachers, Jesus inspired humanity toward higher consciousness and freedom from "sin" (i.e., negativity and karmic debt) with the message that "the kingdom of heaven is within you." NOT SEPARATE AND APART. According to the Gospel of Thomas, Jesus stressed that God "is inside you and outside you. When you know yourselves, then you will be known, and you will understand that you are children of the living Father. But if you do not know yourselves, then you live in poverty, and you are the poverty." Many believe his inner planes name, or spiritual identity, is "Sananda."

Helps with the following: clear reception of divine guidance, faith, forgiveness, healing of any kind, manifestation

Kuthumi

According to Theosophical researchers, Kuthumi is an ascended master whose incarnations included the following: Thutmose III, the sixth pharaoh of Egypt's 18th Dynasty; Pythagoras, the Greek philosopher and mathematician; Pericles, the Athenian statesman; Balthasar, the Magus—believed to have been the King of Ethiopia— who brought frankincense to the infant Jesus; Shah Jahan, a Mughal emperor of India; and lastly, Thakar Singh (b. 1837–d. 1887), a Sikh activist who sought to restore his cousin, Duleep Singh, as Maharaja of the Punjab.

Helps with the following: dedication to one's life purpose, focus, motivation

Melchizedek

Depending on which spiritual text you consult, Melchizedek is either Noah's son, Noah's nephew, Archangel Michael, an early incarnation of Jesus, or an order of divine beings, one of whom materialized as a human 1,973 years before Jesus' birth to teach the concept of one, universal deity and to announce that another Son of God (Jesus) would be born of a woman and become, as the Bible says, "a priest forever in the order of Melchizedek." All of these views intersect on two key points: Melchizedek was 1. a priest-king of Salem, i.e., modern-day Jerusalem and 2. a teacher of Abraham. Hebrews 7:3 further describes him as having "neither beginning of days nor end of life, but made like the Son of God, he remains a priest perpetually." The Tanakh (Jewish Bible) tells of Melchizedek's gift of bread and wine to Abram (Abraham), and it's been said that this offering foreshadowed Jesus's use of bread and wine at the Last Supper.

Helps with the following: balance and harmony of energies (as with color therapy or feng shui), chakra clearing, greater comprehension of spiritual concepts through sacred geometry (described under Archangel Metatron in chapter 3), healing, inner peace, manifestation, protection from psychic attack

Moses

He's known as *Moshe* in Hebrew, but a growing number of scholars believe the name "Moses" was short for a longer one derived from an Egyptian deity; their best guess is Ramoses, meaning "child of Ra" or "Ra is born." Although raised in the Egyptian court, Moses delivered the Hebrews from Egypt and became the most important prophet of Judaism. Christianity, Islam, and other religions, such as the Bahá'í Faith, also regard him as a prophet. Tradition has it that the Torah—the first five books of the Bible's Old Testament—was revealed to Moses on Mount Sinai. The location of that mysterious mountain is still debated, but guesses include Mount Bedr in Saudi Arabia, Mount Catherine in Egypt, and Hashem el-Tarif. Whatever the truth, modern historians believe the Exodus (the Israelites' big exit) took place sometime between 1290 BCE and 1211 BCE. According to the Ascended Master Teachings, Moses reincarnated as Gautama Buddha's foremost disciple, Ananda, and as a medieval Chinese nobleman called Lord Ling.

Helps with the following: courage, faith, dealing with authority figures, leadership, living in "the now"

Mother Mary

Accounts of miraculous conceptions and births exist in a great many cultures. Just one example, from the 14th century BCE, is the nativity scene—including the annunciation, conception, birth, and adoration—of Amenhotep III inscribed on the walls of the Temple at Luxor. Be that as it may, the mother of Jesus (Yeshua) became one of the most beloved women in history. Although the Christian sect of Collyridianism worshipped Mary as a Mother Goddess, the majority of Christians revered her as the mother of their savior, and by extension, the spiritual mother of "the faithful." The Roman Catholic Church gave her titles like the Blessed Virgin Mary, the Queen of Heaven, and the Star of the Sea, and she became a protector of—and mediator for—humanity. Muslim scripture places her above all women of her generation: "Behold! the angels said: 'O Maryam (Mary)! Allah hath purified thee and chosen thee, chosen thee above the women of all nations.'" (Qur'an 3:42) "And she who guarded her chastity, so We breathed into her through our Angel, and We made her and her son a sign for the worlds." (Qur'an 21:91) Many believe Mary works with angels to create miracles, and like the "Eastern" bodhisattva ("enlightened being") Kuan Yin, she epitomizes compassion, mercy, and feminine grace. Marian apparitions have been reported all over the world. Some of the better known sightings occurred in the following locations: Tepeyac, Mexico; Lourdes, France; Fátima, Portugal; the Zeitoun district of Cairo, where thousands of people, including Egyptian President Gamal Abdel Nasser, witnessed the spectacle; and Assiut, Egypt from August 2000 to January 2001, during which time thousands produced photographs or video clips of the recurring event.

Helps with the following: anything related to children and their caretakers, healing, love, prayer, protection

Padre Pio, Saint

"Through the study of books one seeks God; by meditation one finds Him." So stated Pio of Pietrelcina—
born Francesco Forgione—an Italian priest who, despite his own ill health, performed miraculous healings
and became a symbol of hope after the devastation of
World War I. He experienced the stigmata and was
known to levitate, predict the future, and bilocate, appearing on different continents at the same time. He
also had the gift of glossolalia (speaking in tongues)
and often communicated with guardian angels, which
sometimes helped him grant favors and healings before
he was even asked for them. "After my death, I will do
more," he often said. "My real mission will begin after
my death." Just before 2:30 a.m. on September 23, 1968,
he said, "I see two mothers." Then, with his last breath,
he whispered, "Maria!" More than a hundred thousand
people attended his requiem mass, and he was later
canonized by Pope John Paul II. Years before, while
that pope was still a young priest known as Father Karol
Józef Wojtyła, Padre Pio reportedly told him that he
would one day rise to the "highest post in the Church."
Another prediction: in 1959, Padre Pio said, "When the
crypt is blessed, God will call Padre Pio home." September 22, 1968 was the very day the bishop blessed the
crypt which had been made for Padre Pio.

Helps with the following: faith, forgiveness, healing, optimism, prophecy, transcending chronic pain, spiritual growth

Saint-Germain

Not to be confused with a Catholic saint or the colorful Parisian neighborhood, the Comte (Count) de Saint-Germain was an elusive figure who fed the mystery wherever he went. An aristocrat of unknown origin—possibly a son of Francis II Rákóczi, Prince of Transylvania—Saint-Germain was described as a brilliant artist, musician, linguist, alchemist, scientist, inventor, seer, adventurer, and secret agent. Voltaire called him "a man who was never born, who will never die, and who knows everything." Indeed, reports say his physical appearance—which suggested he was between forty and fifty years of age—remained unchanged for more than a century! Many claim he was far older, that he was actually Francis Bacon, who they believe faked his death on Easter Sunday, 1626. Although one account places him in Venice at the end of the 1600s, he burst onto the European social scene around 1740 and hobnobbed with illustrious characters like Jean-Jacques Rousseau, Giacomo Casanova, Anton Mesmer, Prince Charles of Hesse-Kassel, Louis XV, Madame de Pompadour, Marie Antoinette, the Count di Cagliostro, and Catherine the Great. He could supposedly transmute lead into gold and was linked to a number of esoteric societies, including the Rosicrucians, the Illuminati, and the Freemasons. Some say he inspired the Founding Fathers to write the U.S. Declaration of Independence and the Constitution. Apparently, he staged his death yet again on February 27, 1784, because credible accounts place him in a number of locations well after that time.

Helps with the following: courage, direction, dealing with authority figures, perseverance, psychic protection, spiritual alchemy

Serapis Bey

According to the Ascended Master Teachings, Serapis Bey is Chohan of the Fourth (white) Ray of God's purity, harmony, and discipline. His previous incarnations included the Egyptian pharaoh Amenhotep III and the Spartan king Leonidas. It's also believed he lived in the sixth century BCE as the wise philosopher Confucius—known in China as K'ung Fu-Tse—whose teachings were so advanced that they became China's official philosophy for two thousand years. Confucius advocated harmony and divine order within the self, the family, and society as a whole, and he championed what he termed the "golden" rule of reciprocity: "Never impose on others what you would not choose for yourself." Supposedly, in the nineteenth century, Serapis Bey worked with El Morya, Kuthumi, and other ascended masters to institute the Theosophical Society.

Helps with the following: creative endeavors, harmonious relationships (personal and global), harnessing intuition, honesty with oneself and with others, motivation, overcoming addictions, research and reflection

Solomon

According to ancient texts, Solomon—from the Hebrew *Shelomoh* ("peace" or "complete"), also known as *Sulaiman* ("man of peace") in transliterated Arabic—was the third king of the United Monarchy, i.e., the kingdoms of Israel and Judah. He ruled for a period of forty years in the tenth century BCE and is credited with building Jerusalem's first temple, wherein the Ark of the Covenant was kept. Lauded for his wisdom, King Solomon is nevertheless a controversial figure from the Judaic and Christian perspectives. However, modern historians believe political and economic issues— not idolatry—caused the division of his kingdom. Archaeological evidence suggests that ordinary Israelites worshipped God as both Yahweh and his feminine counterpart, Asherah, and that the "Yahweh-only" belief was established much later, during and after the Babylonian Exile. When Solomon honored foreign deities, he was not only consistent with prevailing traditions, but a courteous leader and shrewd politician. The Greek Orthodox Church and Islam consider him a prophet, and Arabic legends extol his skills as a warrior and his love of horses. The Qur'an describes his rule over invisible beings known as the jinn, and *The Testament of Solomon*—compiled between the first and third centuries CE—agrees, describing his use of a magical ring and its five-pointed seal, given to him by Archangel Michael. Both Solomon and his father, King David, were said to understand the language of the birds, and as Kabbalistic adepts, they were privy to many of the world's hidden wonders.

Helps with the following: divine magic, Kabbalah study, keen insight, manifestation, space clearing (of negativity), understanding

Thérèse of Lisieux, Saint

Born Marie-Françoise-Thérèse Martin in 1873, this French Carmelite nun lived only twenty-four years but inspired millions of people—including such diverse figures as Anaïs Nin and Mother Teresa of Calcutta— with her autobiography, *The Story of a Soul*, and her "little way" of seeing God in ordinary events. She herself was greatly inspired by the works of the sixteenth-century Spanish mystic and Catholic saint, John of the Cross. She embodied the magical child archetype and believed that the divine love which creates every unique thing protects and sustains it. For her, the fear of God was an odd concept. "My nature is such that fear makes me recoil," she wrote. "With LOVE, not only do I go forward, I fly." She also asserted, "I have long believed that the Lord is more tender than a mother... Children are always giving trouble, falling down, getting themselves dirty, breaking things—but all this does not shake their parents' love for them." About prayer, she wrote, "I do like a child who does not know how to read; I say very simply to God what I wish to say, without composing beautiful sentences, and He always understands me." She died in 1897 and is reported to have said, "My mission—to make God loved—will begin after my death.

I will spend my heaven doing good on earth. I will let fall a shower of roses." She apparently kept her word. Thousands of miracles—many of which occurred years before she was canonized—have been attributed to her, and throughout World War I, soldiers on both sides of the battlefields described visions of a young nun, who they believed was Thérèse, comforting wounded men during battle. One French pilot even painted her image on his wing! Pope John Paul II declared her a Doctor of the Church in 1997.

Helps with the following: childlike trust, gardening, healing illness or injury, protection from malice, safety of aviators and airline crew, spiritual counseling

Yoganada

Born Mukunda Lal Ghosh on January 5, 1893, Paramahansa Yogananda was an Indian yogi and guru who introduced "westerners" to meditation and Kriya Yoga, which he learned from his own guru, Swami Sri Yukteswar Giri, a disciple of Lahiri Mahasaya, who learned the art directly from Mahavatar Babaji. Like Sri Yukteswar, Yogananda believed in the essential unity of all religions; he also thought that a balance between the bustling activity of the West (an expression of life) and the calm of the East (the enjoyment of life) was necessary. Of miracles, he said, "The so-called miraculous powers of a great master are a natural accompaniment to his exact understanding of subtle laws that operate in the inner cosmos of consciousness." Furthermore,

"Nothing may be truly said to be a 'miracle' except in the profound sense that everything is a miracle." In 1920, he traveled to Boston, Massachusetts as India's delegate to an International Congress of Religious Liberals, and soon after founded the Self-Realization Fellowship (SRF). Thousands attended his lectures, and within a few years, he established an international SRF center in Los Angeles. He briefly returned to India from 1935 to 1936—when Sri Yukteswar honored him with the monastic title of *Paramhansa* (also spelled *paramahansa* and translated as "supreme swan")—but lived the remainder of his life in the U.S. His published works include *In the Sanctuary of the Soul, Man's Eternal Quest, The Divine Romance,* and the bestselling *Autobiography of a Yogi,* which made Harper San Francisco's list of "The 100 Best Spiritual Books of the Century" in 1999. He died on March 7, 1952 at the age of 59.

Helps with the following: all forms of healing, balance, clear communication with God, meditation, unifying religious beliefs, world peace, yoga

God reveals itself in infinite ways—and through diverse individuals like the ascended masters—precisely because it *is* infinite and omnipresent. One source with many faces, each designed to remind us that our true nature is Spirit and we are all one.

If the individuals above piqued your curiosity, there are extensive source materials on them and others believed to be ascended masters. The recommended reading list at the back of this book can get you started.

You can meet the ascended masters through the Meditation for Meeting Angels at the end of chapter 5; just make one or more ascended masters the focus of your intention. Or you can simply contact specific masters by speaking to them—in your mind or out loud—just as you would the angels. As with angelic communication, the easiest way to talk to ascended masters is to speak from your heart and in your own words. There's no right or wrong way to do it. In other words, be yourself.

If you still feel hesitant, here are a couple of examples:

To contact Melchizedek: "Melchizedek, I welcome your powerful presence. Please clear away all negative energies. Transform this situation so that it mirrors the highest spiritual laws and creates the best outcome for everyone concerned. Guide my thoughts, words, and actions concerning (insert problem) and protect me in every way. I trust your wisdom and know you will help me. Thank you."

To contact St. Francis: "St. Francis, please remind me of my original intentions for this lifetime and guide me toward the perfect opportunities to use my God-given talents and abilities. Help me to be a channel for divine energy that will affect the world in positive ways. Thank you."

Refer to the appendix for an alphabetized list of specific needs and ascended masters who can help with them.

8

Other Spirit Guardians and Fairies

Now, hold onto your hat. Our investigation is about to take a fantastic turn. I use the term "fantastic" because some readers might regard the next set of guardians as pure fantasy or highly improbable. Many of you, however, will recognize these beings from personal experience or as something you assumed your child imagined. Whatever your stance may be, please keep an open mind and remember that thousands of people have claimed direct contact with guardians such as these.

I'm talking about elemental beings, elves, fairies, and even mythological creatures like dragons and unicorns.

As D. J. Conway asserts in *Guides, Guardians, and Angels*, "if you are friendly and welcoming to these unique beings, you will soon find you have a constant crowd of them. They are fantastic for raising vibrations within your environment ... And the mythical creatures, especially dragons, are powerful protectors."

Such guardians come from the elemental realm—associated with the elements of nature—and the spirit realm. The former includes elementals, fairies, devas, and dryads, all of which we'll discuss. The latter, of which we've already explored angels and ascended masters, includes both human and animal spirits. Let's delve into both worlds, one at a time.

The Elemental Realm

As a child, I sensed and respected the life force that flows through the natural world, but I was twenty-five before I first glimpsed the auras around plants, and older still when I learned about scientists like Sir Jagdish Chandra Bose and Cleve Backster. Their research showed that plants communicate through chemical and electrical signals, responding to stimuli in a rather sentient way.

If plants—as well as animals—are not only alive but aware, wouldn't they, like humans, receive spiritual assistance? If the universe runs on unconditional love, that love would extend to the whole.

The Talmud addresses this topic: "Every blade of grass has its Angel that bends over it and whispers, 'Grow, grow.'" Auric energy is evident around the grass, but it's only part of the picture. Everything in creation is so be-loved that it has its own guardian. Believe it or not, nature spirits can serve in that capacity.

Many categorize fairies as part of the elemental realm. Others reserve that world for the elements them-selves—earth, air, fire, and water—along with the guard-ians (Watchtowers) and forces (Dragons and Winds) of their corresponding directions: North, South, East, and West. Obviously, nature spirits are hard to pigeon-hole. Encounters with them are highly subjective, but the humans involved always come away with strong im-pressions and a firm belief that these beings are real.

Elementals

Elementals are nature spirits associated with the four el-ements: gnomes are of earth, sylphs of air, salamanders of fire, and undines of water. They are present whenever "magic" is worked, and they receive their orders from devas, divine forces of intelligence which we'll discuss in a bit.

People from a variety of cultures have long sensed nature spirits. Take for example, the Japanese religion of Shinto, which recognizes numerous *kami*—deities and spirits of the natural world—which can be forces of nature or elements of the landscape, e.g., rocks or caves. In *Working with Earth Energies: How to Tap into the Healing Powers of the Natural World*, David Furlong states, "The beings that inhabit these realms are conscious like you and I, although obviously they have a very different way of connecting to the physical world around us."

These nature spirits are attracted to young children and often appear to them. As Furlong asserts, "The child that claims to have seen a 'fairy' may indeed be telling the truth. With a little practice it is quite possible to sense their presence, and if you are lucky, to see them clairvoyantly."

In *How to Meet and Work with Spirit Guides*, Ted Andrews explains that elementals have certain characteristics whereas nature spirits like fairies and elves have distinct personalities. "For example, in any one family there may be a particular characteristic or trait that all of the family members have—a tendency to baldness, thinness, a sharp nose, etc.—but each person in that family will display a 'unique' personality, despite the common characteristic."

Here's a little information on the four types of elementals.

Gnomes

Gnomes are earth elementals. They maintain the solid, physical structure of the planet: rocks, stones, minerals, precious gems, hills, and mountains. They're linked to our "earthy nature," including physical sensations and fertility. They can assist humans with anything concerning growth, whether in a garden or one's inner self. They're also believed to strengthen our endurance and help us attract prosperity. They're usually perceived as male or female dwarves.

Sylphs

Sylphs are air elementals. They're found in everything from a slight breeze to a raging cyclone, and they help us metabolize the air we breathe. They're associated with human creativity, inspiration, and mental development. They're also believed to protect travelers. Their vibration is higher than that of the other three elementals, and their appearance is very like the traditional Tinkerbell image of fairies.

Salamanders

Salamanders are fire elementals. Apparently, you can't even light a match without a salamander being present. They're extremely powerful protectors who spark human passion, motivation, and courage. Their transformative energy can cleanse negativity and aid healing. They've been perceived as heat, balls of light, or lizards.

Undines

Undines (also known as ondines), are water elementals. They're connected to all liquids, even those inside plants, animals, and human beings. They live everywhere where there is water, from tiny drops of rain to fathomless oceans. Linked to human emotion and imagination, they can facilitate healing, purification, empathy, and intuition. They often appear as blurs of color. Reports of mermaids and mermen throughout history are thought to be encounters with these elementals. However, recent mermaid sightings—such as those reported in the Israeli town of Kiryat Yam—and the U.S. National Oceanic and Atmospheric Administration's 1997 "Bloop" recordings fuel continued belief in the existence of merpeople as actual, biological creatures.

I suspect at least one elemental entered our home when my children were three. One night, I dreamed I was sitting cross-legged on the marble floor of a pillared temple. In my lap sat someone I assumed was a boy. Because his back was to me, I couldn't see his face, but he wore the traditional Indian dhoti kurta and a turban. He sang part of a Hindi song I learned in graduate school fifteen years before. Then he turned to face me.

He wasn't a boy at all. His head was half the size of a human child's, yet his features—although devoid of any actual expression—were mature and shriveled. He was, quite literally, a little man.

Using telepathy, he questioned me about the song. *Remember that?*

"Yes," I answered.

I was with you when you learned it, he said.

"Who are you?"

You already know. With those words, he disappeared.

"Where are you?" I asked. Then I woke abruptly.

I was lying on my side in bed, and I sensed a presence at my back. A rush of wind blasted the back of my neck, and a raspy reply filled my left ear.

I am here!

Chill bumps erupted over my entire body. For an instant, I wondered whether my husband was playing a joke. Then I heard the shower running in our bathroom. I turned and, sure enough, found myself "alone" in bed.

Two subsequent events, a few days later, seemed related. The first occurred in the morning before the boys left for preschool. They were playing in the living room while I emptied the dishwasher in the kitchen. Abruptly, their play stopped.

Then Geoffrey spoke up. "Boy, Mommy. Boy."

He pointed and stared down the hall toward the foyer. I turned to look but saw no one.

The second incident happened later that afternoon, shortly after the boys returned home. I was back in the kitchen, and Geoffrey made a beeline for the refrigerator. Suddenly, he stopped short.

"Boy, Mommy," he said, frowning. "No boy. No boy, Mommy."

My arms and the back of my neck might have belonged to a porcupine, for the hairs stood straight up. Maybe I felt what he saw. Or maybe I got chills because of where he saw it.

He stared at a point directly to the right of my head, as if the "boy" hovered beside me.

"No boy," he said, as though giving a command. "No boy, Mommy."

I realized then he wanted our visitor to leave. I was poised to ask a question but never got the chance.

"Bye, boy," he said, waving at the same spot beside me. "Bye."

A second later, he smiled with satisfaction. Then he took my hand and led me from the room.

He never mentioned the "boy" again, and there was no encore performance in my dreams. But the little sage's clothing gave me a clue. Indian folklore has its own correlates to fairies, elves, dwarves, and other creatures from the elemental realm. Even though I knew nothing about them at the time, maybe I met one.

It wasn't the first Indian symbol or guide I'd seen in a dream, and it was no coincidence—way back in graduate school—that the only fellowship available to finance my summer studies was one that required a course in Hindi and Urdu. I've been told that I had at least two past lives in India as a member of the Brahmin caste and a teacher of Hinduism. Perhaps those lifetimes hold the key to my dreamtime visitor's purpose and identity.

Fairies (The Fae)

These are the "little people," although some are reportedly larger than humans. They come in all shapes and sizes, and their classification is a sticky subject ... which seems appropriate, given that many are believed to be shapeshifters!

Some think they're indistinguishable from the elementals: the gnomes, sylphs, salamanders, and undines.

Others argue that the fairy realm is quite distinct from the elemental one.

In *Phenomenon*, Sylvia Browne asserts that fairies, alongside beings such as elves and "mythological" beasts, inhabit the First Level of the Underworld—another dimension, *not* the temporary, illusionary hell some souls create for themselves out of preconditioned fear—which she describes as a mirror image of the Other Side. "Each of them is comprised of seven levels. On the Other Side the levels ascend to the highest possible advancement, which is the seventh. In the Underworld, also called the Seven Lower Levels of Creation, the most highly advanced beings are found on the First Level, and the advancement descends from there."

In *Guides, Guardians, and Angels*, D. J. Conway discusses human-sized fae, the elf warriors, magicians, and mystics who sometimes guard humans. She agrees they are highly advanced, "very close to where you will find angels." They aid and protect those who work magic, and they can on occasion guard humans who are simply out enjoying nature, especially if said humans are spiritually open and aware.

At the very least, the fairy races are caretakers of the natural world, acting in many cases as "guardian angels" to plants and animals. There are so many types that the information could constitute a whole book, so let's just focus on three: flower fairies, leprechauns, and the *aos sí (sídhe)*.

Flower Fairies

Just like flowers, flower fairies come in different sizes, anywhere from two inches to slightly less than a foot high. Wing appearance also varies: some resemble dragonfly wings; others resemble those of butterflies. The smallest among these creatures are sometimes mistaken for dragonflies, butterflies, or fireflies, thanks to the speed with which they flit about natural settings, but those who've glimpsed them stock-still describe their humanlike faces and natural beauty.

Unlike angels, fairies have egos. Accordingly, they make judgments about people and events. In *Fairies 101: an Introduction to Connecting, Working, and Healing with the Fairies and Other Elementals*, Doreen Virtue clarifies that their reputed mischief occurs only when they judge specific humans as hurtful toward animals or the environment. Otherwise, they're friendly beings who help us create or maintain beautiful homes and gardens, artistic inspiration, prosperity, and good health for both ourselves and our pets.

You don't have to be a professional psychic to see these beings. While studying at an English university, one of my friends had a roommate who enjoyed a close relationship with fairies and diminutive elves. Apparently, they would line themselves up around her mantelpiece in a show of support whenever she was feeling low.

My own children reported seeing "little angels," whom they later called "fairies," in and around our potted garden from the time they were three. I almost wrote it off as active imagination, but time and again, they validated each other's stories by independently sharing identical details about the fairies' physical appearance, personalities, and locations inside and outside of our house. When two children—each separate from the other, with no knowledge of the other's actions—point to the same spot and give matching descriptions of what's there, you think twice.

Leprechauns

Respect for all classes of "faerie folk" is widespread in Ireland, but no fairy is more identified with the Emerald Isle than the leprechaun (Middle Irish *luchorpán,* "small body"). Place names like Poulaluppercadaun ("pool of the leprechaun") near Killorglin in County Kerry and Knocknalooricaun ("hill of the leprechauns") near Lismore in County Waterford show the prevalence of this character in the Irish mindset. There's even a website, www.irelandseye.com, which has set up a live "leprechaun fairy watch webcam" in a Tipperary field.

Leprechauns are believed to be guardians of ancient treasure, some of which was purportedly left by Viking invaders. Some believe they encourage humans to think thoughts of abundance which ultimately attract wealth. In *Fairies 101,* Doreen Virtue describes them as supportive of humans they admire, yet impish toward those they don't. She believes they're drawn to musicians and environmentalists and sometimes act as personal spirit guides. "Because they're large and close to the earth's density," she explains, "leprechauns are among the easiest of the elementals to see with your physical eyes, especially if you visit the Irish countryside."

My paternal great-grandfather, Michael—who emigrated from Ireland in 1914—encountered a leprechaun one night as he plodded home. The street was deserted, so he was surprised by the sudden appearance of a "little man" padding toward him on top of a stone wall. Something about the man made him uneasy, so Michael diverted his gaze to the ground. A moment later, he felt compelled to look up, and when he did, the man was gone. Then a flicker of movement on the other side of the street caught Michael's eye.

There on the opposite stone wall stood the little man, staring at him. He'd traversed the distance in the blink of an eye. More nervous than ever, Michael averted his gaze again. Seconds later, he glanced up, but the man had vanished for good.

My great-grandfather had no doubt he'd seen a leprechaun. According to legend, if you keep your eye on a leprechaun, he can't escape, but the minute you look away, he disappears. Michael's experience was right in line with this belief, and the memory of it stayed with him the rest of his life.

Aos Sí (Sídhe)

Tradition holds that the *aos sí* (from *aes sídhe*, "people of the mounds") are descended from the *Tuatha Dé Danann*, ("people of the goddess Danu") a people who settled in ancient Ireland but ultimately retreated to another dimension, referred to as either the otherworld or the underworld. Large, wingless, and humanoid, they are comparable to J. R. R. Tolkien's version of elves and are one of many next-door—next-dimension—neighbors.

Many trees and mounds are thought to be under their protection. Nowadays, the name for their dwelling places has become so synonymous with their race that most English speakers simply refer to them as "the Sidhe" (pronounced *shee*).

Far from the stereotypical "little people," they're often described as tall, handsome, and richly dressed. Even St. Patrick was said to have encountered one: a beautiful young woman wearing a green mantle and a golden crown. The Colloquy with the Ancients describes her as being "of the Tuatha Dé Danann, who are unfading and whose duration is perennial."

A number of *sídhe* (the places, not the people!) have been identified as ancient burial mounds. These discoveries—together with oral history and information recorded in the Annals of the Four Masters and *The Book of Invasions*—support the theory that the aos sí occupied pre-Celtic Ireland.

One possible member of the aos sí is the female, familial guardian regarded as a howling harbinger of death. She's known the world over as the banshee, which is the Anglicized version of *bean sídhe* ("woman of the fairy mound"), yet she's more like a spirit than the diminutive fairies of European lore.

The banshee can appear as a beautiful maiden, a dignified matron, or a crone—the triune aspects of The Morrigan, the Celtic goddess of war, fate, and death—with long hair and long, flowing robes to match. Her wail or keen always foretells a death in the family. In the Scottish tradition, the *bean nighe* ("washer woman") is seen washing the blood-soaked clothes, or in times past, the armor of the doomed individual.

Because of my Irish heritage, you might feel a story coming on ... and you'd be right! As you'd expect, it involves my great-grandfather, Michael.

One night, he and his mates were enjoying a round of drinks at the local pub. After a time, the door swung open, and another friend burst into the room. He was wild-eyed, drawn, and out of breath. Michael ushered him over to their table, and the man dropped to a chair and raked a hand through his disheveled hair.

"What is it?" they asked him.

Their friend cast a glance over his shoulder, then blurted out his tale. He hadn't slept in days. He'd stolen the golden comb from a banshee, and she was chasing him to reclaim it.

They looked at one another and scratched their heads, until the man opened his coat. Popping up from the inside pocket was a sparkling, gold comb.

Suddenly, he jumped from his chair. "Do you hear that?" he asked.

The others shook their heads as one.

"She's here," the man cried. "She's found me."

He broke from the group and darted out of the pub. The next morning, he was found dead, spread out on his back, fully dressed, atop his perfectly made bed. His coat lay open, and his attire was the same as the previous evening in all ways but one. The golden comb was gone.

Tradition holds that banshees—like mermaids—possess either gold or silver combs, which they sometimes place on the ground to attract a human's attention. Then they spirit the person away to another dimension. When you think about it, that's a pretty accurate description of death.

Accounts of banshees, such as the one my great-grandfather told, go a long way toward scaring the bejeezus out of believers, but the banshee is really a benevolent spirit. Like it or not, death is a natural, transformative part of our existence. The banshee's cry prepares a family—or an individual—for what's to come and can actually help those left behind through the grieving process.

Devas

Considered part of both the angelic and elemental kingdoms, devas are living forces that hold in their consciousness the blueprint of every created thing. The word "deva" (pronounced "day-va") comes from the Sanskrit root *div,* meaning "to shine" or "become bright." So a deva is a "shining one" who works behind the scenes, shifting and guarding the physical form—of a plant, a stone, even a bodily organ—with an instinctive knowledge of archetypal and cosmic patterns, connections, and harmonies. Put simply, devas are the architects of natural growth.

Bethelda, the angel who communicated with Geoffrey Hodson, had this to say: "In your scientific studies, as they take you deeper into the super-physical realms, be ever observant of our place in the manipulation and adjustment of Nature's forces. Behind every phenomenon, you will find a member of our race... So long as the presence of our invisible hosts is ignored by science there will be gaps in their knowledge, gaps which can only be filled by a comprehension of our place in the scheme of things."

As the divine intelligence behind "blue-collar" nature spirits (e.g., fairies), a deva can oversee a single tree or a whole forest. Large collectives of devas have been worshipped as gods and goddesses; the Celtic goddess Druantia, the Finnish goddess Mielikki, the Incan goddess Pachamama, the Roman god Faunus, and the well-known, multicultural Green Man are some examples. The planetary deva or devi (the feminine form of the word) is known as Gaia, the Earth Mother, or "Mother Nature."

Devas also work with humans—giving advice on planting, fertilizing, watering, etc.—as in the communities of Perelandra in Virginia and Findhorn in Scotland. During the drought disaster of 1986, Perelandra's flowers and vegetables flourished without added moisture and astounded neighbors, one of whom remarked, "It's not normal." Findhorn's garden—which included 42-pound cabbages in the early days (1960s and '70s)—stunned visiting horticulturists and soil experts who eventually had to accept the possibility of "angelic" cooperation. In 1997, after a number of official collaborations, the United Nations formally recognized the Findhorn Foundation as a Non-Government Organization. Since then, Findhorn has participated in UN conferences around the world.

Dryads

Some believe that tree spirits—what the ancient Greeks called dryads—are devas. Others distinguish between the two. Regardless of the name or classification we give them, tree spirits have been revered for millennia by numerous cultures. They certainly inspired the Druids, particularly with the Ogham script of ancient Ireland. For my part, I suspect that tree spirits introduced me to the elemental realm.

When I was a child, my favorite trees were oaks draped in Spanish moss, and if I stood very close and very still, they seemed to whisper to me of ancient powers and buried wisdom. But things really got interesting when I studied at a folkhögskola in Sweden as an adult. Shortly after my twenty-fifth birthday, a fellow student and friend revealed a long kept secret.

"Back home in Russia, I became very ill," she said. "For a long time, I had no strength and no hope of getting better. I was at my wits' end until I met a woman who was a psychic and a healer. She told me about nature spirits, especially the ones that inhabit trees. She taught me how to ask for their help and how to draw energy from them."

Her sincerity was obvious. She had no doubt the energy had healed her. In essence and in effect, the trees saved her life. I didn't know it then, but this principle of energy exchange with nature—trees, in particular—would reappear in my life in less than a month, when my intuition prompted me to travel to the English town of Glastonbury.

The town enchanted me from the get-go, and I made the most of my limited time there. I explored the abbey ruins, climbed the Tor, and tasted the healing waters of Chalice Well.

My visit shifted into high gear when I met a group of locals at a nearby pub. We discussed a number of topics, from Arthurian legend to crop circles. They told me about the Gog and Magog, two great oaks which were supposed relics of a Druidic grove that ascended Glastonbury Tor. The natives viewed the trees as male and female, respectively, and one was apparently ill.

The hours and hypotheses waxed with the moon until a handful of people proposed a midnight trek to the site of the ancient oaks. They felt an urgent need to transmit healing energy to the ailing tree, and they invited me to tag along.

My best friend in Sweden had spoken of extracting energy from trees; now others intended to give. In the spirit of adventure, I agreed to go.

By the moon's glow, we hoofed it over a patchwork quilt of fields and fences to the proper spot. The massive pair of oaks stretched gnarled and knobby branches high into the darkness, and their wizened features demanded respect even as they conjured images of a mystic past.

As I drew closer, an overwhelming sense of déjà vu flooded into me. Either I'd been there before, or I'd approached oaks somewhere else in a reverent, ritual manner. As I mentioned before, they were my favorite trees during childhood, but the feeling that swept through me now was exceptional and evocative. The exact time and circumstances were shrouded, but I knew it was long ago.

At present, our little lot surrounded the sick tree and clasped hands. One of the women led us in prayer; then as we began to circle the tree, she uttered an incantation. When she fell silent, we moved forward and placed our hands on the rough, dry bark.

I closed my eyes and sensed that the tree was both sentinel and sage. Within seconds, intense love welled up in my chest, and I seemed to become a conduit. An unseen force entered the top of my head and surged into my heart, crystallizing as a warm, tingling sensation. I directed it down my arms and into my hands, then sent it into the tree. I maintained both flow and focus for several minutes until—through some nameless indicator—I felt the transfer was complete. Then I opened my eyes and watched the others do the same. As one, we stepped away.

My hands were still humming as we turned to leave the site, so I shook them and rubbed my palms on my legs. Suddenly, an insight seized me. The woman who'd spoken and one of the men seemed familiar with the healing ceremony, but the rest of us had followed instinct. Without instruction or hesitation, we'd simply known what to do.

Did we channel ancestral knowledge? Recall ritual from a past life? Or did devic forces direct us? Your guess is as good as mine, but one thing's sure: I'll never forget the magic of that night, or doubt the existence of tree spirits.

The Spirit Realm

Guardians from the world of spirit come in many forms, for many reasons. Let's explore them.

Human Spirits

Ancestors

Ancestors can be forerunners—e.g., predecessors in the development of an art form—or distant relations from whom you're descended. As forerunners, they might have mastered the art or sphere within which you work: math, science, agriculture, medicine, art, music, writing, etc. Even when they didn't achieve mastery, they still might be interested in the advancement of that area. As spirit guardians, they watch over your projects and your progress to foster a positive outcome.

In *Guides, Guardians, and Angels*, D. J. Conway affirms that such guardians can include ancient warriors and magicians who occasionally help out. While their presence isn't continuous, they can be with us in an instant, whether we call on them through thought or speech.

Guardian ancestors might also be predecessors in the sense that they faced challenges similar to yours when they were human. Because you share a common experience, they are drawn to your side. At such times, their desire to serve what Conway calls "spiritual justice" moves them to help you. These ancestors of experience might never be seen, but as Conway notes, they "send strong intuitive signals to make you cautious or more alert to life and to upcoming, difficult events."

When ancestors are actually related to you, they might become guardians because they have a particular interest in the progression of their lineage. Right around my twins' first birthday, I chatted with a gifted psychic who didn't know me from Eve, yet she revealed the steady presence of one such ancestor.

"Besides angels and guides, you've got lots of help taking care of your boys," she said. "You may not see them, but the boys do. One female spirit is around them all the time. Do you know an 'Annie'?"

I searched my memory for someone with that name but came up empty-handed. Later that day, I mentioned it to my mother.

"That's Aunt Annie," she said. "She was Flo and Ethel's mother."

Florence and Ethel—my grandmother's first cousins—were spinster sisters whose house had become my parents' second home. I'd never heard their mother's name, but as soon as my mom spoke of her, a memory stirred.

While I was pregnant with the boys, Dan and I visited my parents and slept in the room where Florence, her brother, and Annie had all died. Around 2:00 a.m., I awoke with a strong and immediate sense that someone besides Dan was in the room, watching me. The presence felt feminine and benevolent, and I was certain my pregnancy had piqued her interest. Now, after the psychic's claims, I suspected it was Annie. I also connected her with a thirty-something, dark-haired woman I'd seen in my dreams for years. The dream woman's name? Anya.

Deceased Loved Ones

We might miss deceased loved ones, but they don't miss us. They're around us all the time—literally a thought away—and quite aware of what we're up to. Oftentimes, they know before we do about upcoming events, so it's little wonder they can also serve as guardians.

All of us will grieve the death of a loved one someday, if we haven't done so already. I'd like to share the events surrounding the death of my maternal grandfather in the hope that they'll provide comfort and greater awareness. May they remind you, when the time comes, that the "deceased" is very much alive, watching and sometimes guarding from a dimension right alongside our own.

My grandfather, Poppy, suffered from Alzheimer's, and soon after the death of his wife, Nanny, he lay withered and weak in a nursing home. My parents were three states away when his health suddenly plummeted. By the time they reached the nursing home, he was comatose and hadn't spoken for days.

My mother rushed into his room and took his hand. "Poppy, I love you," she said.

Her presence revived him. "I love you too," he replied.

Not only did he speak, but he recognized her. She stayed in his room from that point on, and he alternated between sleeping and waking.

Two days later, throughout the day, Poppy's gaze darted around the room and up to the ceiling. He repeatedly raised his arms toward what he saw.

The next day, my mom, her best friend, and the nurse all witnessed an incredible reunion. Something unseen lifted Poppy and held him so he sat up in bed. He could never have accomplished the feat on his own. The movement was too quick, and his muscles were dormant.

Poppy's face transformed into an expression of intense love, and my mother was certain of his visitor's identity. He was gazing upon the person he loved most in the world: Nanny.

The next morning and afternoon, seven hawks circled outside Poppy's window, perhaps as an omen signifying the seven levels of the Other Side, his destination. His time had come; still, he hung on. Toward the end of the day, my mother grabbed the phone. Instinct told her

Poppy needed to hear from his other daughter, so she called her sister and held the phone to her father's ear.

"It's okay to go, Poppy," my aunt said.

"Bye-bye," he said. They were the only words he'd spoken—besides "I love you too"—for nine days.

Two hours later, he died. It was five months to the day after his wife's death.

Two days later, Connor and Geoffrey, who were two at the time, woke me and Dan in the middle of the night. When we rushed into their bedroom, they were crying and staring at the same corner of the room they'd indicated during a similar incident the night Nanny died.

"Mommy, grandma, grandpa," Connor said through his tears. "Mommy, grandma, grandpa!"

The energy in the room was palpable. I could almost hear my grandfather's voice.

Don't be afraid. We're your mommy's grandma and grandpa.

Two weeks later, we spent the weekend at my parents' house. A couple of times, the boys' gazes flew to my mother's side.

Both of them looked, but it was Geoffrey who spoke. "Poppy," he said, pointing.

Later, my mom, Dan, and I were talking by the pool. Close by, the boys played with toys in their high chairs.

"No, no, Poppy," said Geoffrey, his voice adamant. "Light on."

He glanced to his side while his hands fiddled with a Spiderman action figure. "No light off, Poppy," he continued. "Light ON."

"Did he just say what I think he said?" I asked Dan, who was gaping at Geoffrey.

"What?" my mother questioned.

"I think he was talking to Poppy," I said.

Geoffrey lifted his gaze to a point about nine feet high, right beside the pool. "Poppy," he said, "Why are you flying?"

My mother raised her eyebrows. "Now I heard that," she said.

On our return home, Geoffrey scampered into the house and halted in front of the Christmas tree. "Poppy," he said with a grin.

A minute later—by which time Geoffrey ignored the tree—Connor scuttled into the living room. He stopped and stared at the same spot his brother had.

"Poppy," he said, smiling.

Apparently, my grandfather tagged along for our journey home.

Four months later, my mom experienced her own series of miracles which reinforced her belief that her parents weren't just together, but still kept an eye on her. For their forty-second wedding anniversary, she and my dad took a nineteen-day trip to Croatia and Slovenia.

Every morning of the trip, she felt an urge to look out of their hotel window. For seventeen out of the nineteen days, a bird perched right outside the window or balcony and peered into their room. She got the impression each time that it was a male bird.

That's Poppy, she thought.

After a bit, a second bird came, seemingly the female. *And there's Nanny,* she thought.

One bird always came first; the other followed a few minutes later. There were different types of birds—doves, chickens, little brown birds, etc.—each day but always two of the same kind. They arrived early in the morning and stayed all day, constantly looking into or toward the hotel room. Even when my parents went sightseeing late into night, the birds were waiting when they returned to the hotel. Then, once my parents were ready for bed, the birds flew away.

The two days of the trip which didn't include birds involved cats. Again, one came first and the other followed shortly thereafter. Both were the same breed of cat, and both times, they stayed all day, looking in on my parents.

My mom called me to share the events once they returned to the States. "I knew my parents were with me through the entire trip," she said. "I felt like they were my guardian angels."

I believed every word of her story, and we both recognized the significance of the messengers my grandparents sent. Their whole lives, their favorite animals were cats and birds.

As a postscript, my parents recently returned from a six-week European river cruise, and a similar phenomenon happened every single day. Do the math. That's forty-two days in a row! First, one bird showed up. Then a second, always of the same species, joined it. In pairs, the birds stayed near my mother for long periods of time, all the while looking into her eyes. The only difference was that this time, the animals involved—eagles, pigeons, seagulls, swans, etc.—were strictly birds.

Animal Spirits

No mention of guardians would be complete without listing animal spirits among their rank. Deceased pets sometimes hang around their owners, and they've been known to make dreamtime visits and to warn humans of danger. Familiars, magical helpers which are animals in physical or astral (spirit) form, can also warn humans of danger and defend them when trouble occurs. (More about familiars in chapter 10.) But by and large, when people speak of animal guardians, they mean totem animals—also called power animals or animal allies—who guide and protect us throughout our lives.

In *Guides, Guardians, and Angels*, D. J. Conway states, "You may find that at critical moments you feel the presence of a powerful animal (mythical or otherwise). They will infuse your aura and mind with whatever qualities you need to protect yourself, as well as projecting their personal defensive feeling directly at whatever or whoever is making you feel threatened."

Not only might *you* pick up on this animal, but *others* might as well. One night, when my sons were four, I lost my temper after two hours(!) of struggling to get them to go to sleep. Immediately after I yelled, Geoffrey asked me why "the wolf"—whom the boys had seen on several occasions, including happy ones—had just appeared, and Connor asked me if it was going to bite them. They saw the animal as plain as day.

When it comes to animal guardians, no species is off limits. Mammals, reptiles, birds, insects, arachnids, and even extinct or mythological beasts: all are potential totems. If you feel inexplicably drawn to one animal and/or repeatedly encounter it in dreams or the waking world, there's a good chance you're connecting with your totem.

The word "totem" derives from the Ojibwe root *-oode-* which refers to kinship. In fact, the Ojibwe people were divided into clans called *doodem* named after different animals. The totem poles among the Native American and First Nations clans are heraldic posts which recount family stories, commemorate special occasions, and sometimes represent shamanic powers. In diverse cultures around the world, a totem was/is any element, animal, plant, or other object—natural or supernatural—whose energy and characteristics provide meaning for an individual or a group. The term has evolved to encompass a broad spectrum of spectral guardians who don't require any particular pedigree of their charges.

Some think totems are familial guardian spirits; others regard them as personal. Many believe they can be both. Some believe you must invoke a totem's protection; others shake their heads and stress that totems choose *you*. Still others insist you can "claim" a totem only if you belong to a North American aboriginal family, but the soul's immortality—not to mention the oneness of creation—smudges all lines of division.

During our various incarnations, we inhabit a variety of races and cultures. A person who's Caucasian this time around might well have been Native American in another life, or in several lives. For that matter, the Celts and other shamanic cultures had/have traditions of animal allies or power animals as rich as any other. Spiritual bonds—however far they stretch—are powerful magnets. Whether human or animal, collective or individual, spirits from other lifetimes affect our present lives. Regardless of our level of awareness, they follow our progress and sometimes pop in for visits.

The subject of totem animals is in itself a whole book, and each animal has its own symbolism. One great source of information on this subject is Ted Andrews's *Animal-Speak*. We'll also talk more about totems in the chapter 10. For now, the least you should know is that we all have at least one animal from the realm of spirit that guards and nurtures us from birth until death. And once we make that "final" transition, they're among the first spirits to welcome us Home.

As you can see, the everyday world is a lot more magical than many suppose; it's also more populated! We can ignore that fact, fear it, or welcome a vast spectrum of possibilities. Each of us has at least one guardian angel, but other spirits—which may include ascended masters, elementals, fairies, devas, ancestors, deceased loved ones, and animals—guard and guide us as well.

The following is a meditation designed to help you meet these unique guardians, one by one or possibly several at once, and you can use the same comfortable room you envisioned for the previous meditation. Please see the meditation section in chapter 5 for specific instructions on the three preparatory steps: 1. state your intention for the meditation; 2. perform a quick grounding and cleansing exercise; 3. start the meditation.

Meditation for Meeting Guardians

Picture yourself in your comfortable room, standing in front of a closed window that's darkened by the night. On the windowsill sits a candlestick which holds a white candle. It will serve as a focal point for you and a beacon for the guardian(s) your intention summons. You light the candle, and a cozy glow fills the room.

You stare at the candle's flame, and its color suddenly shifts to a deep red. A minute later, it takes on a vivid, orange tint. Soon it becomes a cheerful yellow, then a bright green, followed by a peaceful blue. Moments later, the flame begins to alternate between indigo and violet. Then both colors are present, weaving in and out of one another in a soundless dance.

All at once, you sense that the guardian you summoned is outside, just beyond the wall. Its goodwill and anticipation are palpable, and you know it needs no door or window to enter. The candlelight flickers and turns into the brilliant, white color associated with powerful love and protection. You spot movement out of the corner of your eye and realize your guardian has joined you. Turn now and see who it is.

Notice your guardian's appearance. Is it male or female? A human spirit? An animal spirit? Or does it belong to a fairy race? Ask its name and how long it has been with you. You can continue with questions or invite it to tell you whatever it deems important. Keep in mind it might communicate through symbols, or show you an answer instead of telling you. You might also move about the room together or go anywhere/do anything that feels comfortable to you. If you do leave the room, simply return here afterwards.

When you're ready for your guardian to slip back into invisibility, tell it goodbye and watch it disappear. Walk to the window and blow out the candle.

(End of meditation)

Take a few deep breaths and open your eyes. Reflect on your experience and, if you want to keep a record, write down everything you remember about the guardian(s) you encountered and what you learned.

9

Spirit Guides

You will have a number of spirit guides throughout your life. They can change as you grow spiritually, and most come and go as needed, but at least one—your main guide—attends you for life. But what exactly is a spirit guide?

A Spirit Guide Isn't:

An angel: Angels can appear to us in human form, but they don't incarnate as human beings. Our guides, on the other hand, have lived as humans before. It's necessary training for the job; to walk in another's shoes is to fully comprehend the toil of the trek.

A deceased person you knew in this lifetime: Such spirits can surround, support, and even advise you, but they are not actual guides. Your main guide is someone you knew and made great plans with on the Other Side before you were born.

A Spirit Guide Is:

A loving spirit who helps and encourages you along your chosen path: A spirit guide can come from any culture and appear as a member of any race, regardless of yours. He/she is truly invested in your spiritual progress and serves as a teacher, moral compass, and cheerleader all in one. In *Guides, Guardians, and Angels*, D. J. Conway concurs, describing spirit guides as "teachers in everything from ethics and outlook on life to actual studies in astral schools and more." They're the last to wish us "bon voyage" before we incarnate and our steady support while we're here. When we return to the Other Side, they're ready and waiting to help us understand our earthly experiences.

When I mentioned spiritual bonds in the last chapter, I wasn't kidding about their strength. Oftentimes, spirit guides are past-life friends, past-life family, or someone who's been both. On the Other Side, our guides can number among our best friends; they can also be spirits whose company isn't the coziest but whose indomitable will we trusted to kick us in the butt whenever we might need it. Let's face it: most of us could use a well-placed kick toward our goals from time to time.

Those goals originated with the chosen path I mentioned before. Who chooses the path? You do, and your main spirit guide is right by your side when you choose it. Some call it the "life plan"; others refer to it as "the chart."

The Chart

Each of us chose the life we're living now. We picked our family, friends, lovers, acquaintances, and enemies, and they picked us, too. We also selected our professions, illnesses, challenges, goals, and the exact place, date, and time we were born. We created those elements with our free will, and we use that same will to postpone, prolong, mold, and modify events. *At the soul level, we are infinite choice-makers... before, during, and after each lifetime.*

Our prebirth choices for a specific lifetime comprise the chart, which provides a kind of road map or guideline. Ultimately, it allows us to learn, grow, and serve. In *Phenomenon*, Sylvia Browne explains the need for such a chart: "Just as we would never head off to college without deciding which college would serve us best, what courses we'll need, where and with whom we should live, and countless other details to give ourselves the best odds upfront of what we want to accomplish, we wouldn't dream of coming to earth unprepared."

We often make sacred contracts with others preparing to incarnate, agreeing to play specific roles—even if those roles will be difficult or distasteful to perform—for the sake of their spiritual growth and ours. These contracts are responsible for many of the crazy and tragic events we experience in any given lifetime.

Our euphoric state of mind while writing the chart also contributes to the drama. Remember, the Other Side is our true home, and its very fiber is unceasing, unconditional love. In that environment, our enthusiasm, courage, and confidence run the show. As Browne says, "Writing our chart in that state of mind is a little like going to the grocery store on an empty stomach—it's not exactly a recipe for restraint. However challenging your life is, I promise you were in the process of planning something even rougher for yourself until your Spirit Guide, who's lived on earth at least once and hasn't forgotten what it's like, persuaded you into doing something a little more realistic."

Our memory of the game plan or chart is vague, if not void, while we inhabit human bodies, but our guides know every detail. They're our great reminders, trusted allies, and loyal companions. They accepted the job with a sacred promise. Then they were locked in for the ride and all of the ups and downs it entails. That may sound like a herculean task, but most of us will serve—or have served—as guides ourselves.

When life gets tough, our spirit guides can ease the burden by arranging other options for us. In addition, they can appeal to the Council, as D. J. Conway explains in *Guides, Guardians, and Angels*, to soften or terminate karmic lessons, if we've learned them.

The Council

After that last sentence, you might be wondering what or who "the Council" is. It's a group of eighteen male and female beings who, like angels, never incarnate. Sometimes called "the Elders," they are so spiritually advanced that they basically represent God's voice on the Other Side. They wear long, flowing robes and have mature, yet unlined, faces. The men have silver-white beards, while the women have long, straight, silver-white hair.

Before we incarnate in any lifetime, we present our charts to the Council for advice and approval. Then, based on the challenges we've charted, the Council assigns specific angels to watch over us until we arrive back on the Other Side.

What Spirit Guides Do

You might have noticed the number of times I mentioned guides long before we got to this chapter. That's because guides do many of the things angels do and communicate with us in similar ways. Of course, you can't sit around and expect your guides to do everything for you. As Ted Andrews observes in *How to Meet and Work with Spirit Guides*, "spirit guides help those who help themselves."

Their help is invaluable. When you suspect or *know* they're giving you a message, LISTEN! They studied you in depth before you ever left the Other Side. They're familiar with the minute details of your current chart, as well as the charts from your other lives. They can also access the charts of everyone around you, not to mention the akashic records.

When otherwise engaged, they still listen out for you. Think of a mother who's busy in the kitchen but can see and hear her children in the next room; her awareness of them is continuous. And being spirits, guides can bilocate at will.

Like angels, spirit guides are responsible for much of what we call intuition. They communicate with us through infused knowledge and telepathy, so be aware when thoughts hit you "out of the blue," especially if the words, perspective, and/or tone of voice aren't yours.

When a friend of mine was heartbroken and sobbing over a breakup, an abrupt message popped into her head.

Everything will be okay. Things are not finished. Get back to being you, and he will return.

Even though she'd been bawling a moment before, the sudden, soothing message immediately calmed her, and she knew everything would be all right. She believes the message came from her spirit guide.

Spirit guides communicate with others around us in precisely the same way, which is why a friend or colleague might give you the exact same advice you "intuited" on your own. In addition, our guides interact with other people's guides, so there's a lot of information swapping behind the scenes!

Telepathy flows both ways, so you can mentally ask or tell your guides anything you want. When you're alone, you can either say it out loud, or if you're not in the mood to be demure, you can scream it to the heavens. Remember, other spirits feel the pull of your spirit on theirs because everything is connected on that level. When people say, "I won't be there, but I'll be with you in spirit," they're actually speaking the truth. Thought is so magnetic that when they think of you—or you think about them—a part of their spirit is there, with you.

If you're not sure where to begin, start with your main guide. Ask him/her to join you, and take a few deep breaths to quiet your mind. Then ask for a name and listen. If a name leaps to mind, awesome! If not, never fear! You can use whatever name you choose to communicate with your guide: Mary, Mark, Methuse-lah—or Mango-peach, for that matter. Anything goes, and your guide won't mind a bit.

Our spirit guides know the human condition from the inside out and are quite familiar with the veil that shields us from our memories of the Other Side and the totality of our existence. They'll just be grateful you acknowledged them and ready to give you guidance.

Keep in mind that guides, like angels, can warn us of danger and suggest alternatives, but they will never interfere with our free will. We might wish they could intervene, especially when we make mistakes that in hindsight

seem obvious. But freedom is also an amazing gift, necessary for every soul's progression along the spiritual path;
in other words, the evolution of the spirit.

The Evolution of the Spirit

When I was twenty-one, my mother and I visited the
spiritualist community of Cassadaga, Florida. The psychic we consulted was dead-on about a number of things.
After a time, she grabbed a pencil and pad and sketched
the face of one of my "spirit guides." It was the first time
I'd heard the term. Slowly, the outline on the paper became a face, which soon exhibited male features.

"This is one guide I pick up around you," the psychic
said, reaching for a piece of flesh-toned chalk. "His name
is Jacques, and he was an archaeologist in nineteenth-
century France. He supports your seeker personality, and
he keeps showing me an image of digging. It's as if you're
meant to discover something important. It doesn't seem
like an archaeological find, but for you, it might as well
be gold."

What the soul seeks, it finds. A crusty prospector
might say, "There's gold in them thar lives...for all o'
ye!" Indeed, there is. We're talking about spiritual treasure: insight and experience which transform the base
metal of your material existence into the dazzling gold
of your highest potential.

I'm not "digging" here alone, and neither are you.
Spirit guides recognize and encourage such alchemy.
They're evolving, too. In fact, spiritual evolution may

be the point of this whole exercise called life, not just in the third dimension, but in all dimensions.

Just How Close Are Our Guides?

They're closer than you might think! I can best illustrate this intimacy by sharing a few memories, all of which involve a single guide.

When Connor and Geoffrey were three years old, I stayed up late one night to watch TV. Dan was upstairs in bed, but I remained glued to a program on psychic children. Much of the reported phenomena reminded me of my own kids.

My gaze was riveted to the screen, especially when the show introduced twins who'd become professional psychics as adults. It was during that segment I noticed—out of the corner of my eye—what I assumed was Dan near the bottom of the stairs.

"This is incredible," I said out loud. "I ought to contact them."

When "Dan" didn't answer, I spoke again. "Maybe they could give me some advice. The boys chose us to be their parents, and I want us to do the best job we can. What do you—"

I turned in midspeech as a commercial interrupted the program. Then I gaped at the empty stairwell.

I'd been positive someone stood there. I saw the outline of the body. It faced me. It watched me. It listened to me, for crying out loud. In terms of energy, its presence was as tangible as any of flesh and blood.

It felt weird to pass through a space that might still be occupied, but I hurried up the stairs. Dan was lying in bed, moaning as he resurfaced from the depths of sleep.

"Huh?" he grunted in greeting.

"I feel ridiculous even asking this," I said. "You weren't on the stairs a minute ago, were you?"

"No," he replied. "Why?"

"I could've sworn you were there," I explained, "but I guess it was someone else."

Only then, as I started back down the stairs, did I consider my visitor's height. Why it hadn't struck me before is beyond comprehension, but the fact remained: the figure was equal to Dan in stature, if you began measuring about three feet above the appropriate step.

I recalled reading about the difference between ghosts and spirits. Ghosts exist at a higher vibrational frequency than we do but are still earthbound; thus they stand alongside us at ground level. But, as Sylvia Browne explains in *Phenomenon*, spirits have passed through the tunnel and made it to the Other Side, which is approximately three feet above our ground level. Most often, when spirits are described as "floating," they're really just moving along their dimension's ground level.

If that was true, the being in the stairwell must've been either a spirit or an angel. At nine feet plus, it wasn't human.

Soon after that night, I contacted the psychic duo from the TV program for a phone reading. Among other things, they told me I had a spirit guide named Michel, or Michelle.

As I hung up the phone, I pondered one point in particular: was the guide a man or a woman?

Michel or Michelle? I asked in my mind.

Like lightning and crystal clear, I received a mental image of the correct spelling: M-I-C-H-E-L.

"Oh," I said aloud, startled by the strength of an answer I hadn't expected to receive. I felt foolish talking to what appeared to be a vacant room, but I continued. "Well, here's a request. I'd like to know more about you. Whatever way you think is best is fine with me."

That night, I dreamed I was in Ireland. I strolled into a pub and navigated around tables, chairs, and revelers who didn't even notice I was there. Only one man saw me, and he stood in a doorway at the back of the room.

He was a little taller than me. His auburn hair was cut short, but not so short as to hide its natural wave. His eyes were a deep blue, and they bore into mine as I approached. I don't recall him blinking ... at all. But he smiled when I stopped in front of him.

I love you, he said without words.

And I love you, I answered in the same way.

Our love is beyond measure, he continued, *and where you go, I will follow. Trust me. I will see you safely home.*

We embraced. Then my hand slid into his, and we left the pub together.

We glided down a winding road lined with aged stone walls. A throng of people celebrated some festival

I couldn't identify in an emerald green field to our left. But they and every passerby on the street ignored us.

After a time, we entered a modern building, and I noticed a women's restroom at the end of the hall.

Just a second, I told my companion. *I'll be right back.*

I entered the bathroom. Every stall was occupied, so I took my place at the end of a long line of women.

For some reason, I looked to my right. There, within the yard's distance between me and the wall, was my blue-eyed redhead.

You see? he said. *I'm even here.*

Obviously, I replied. *But why in the name of heaven should you be in a bathroom?*

You just said it, he answered. *I'm here in the name of heaven. I'm wherever you need me to be.*

Abruptly, I awoke ... with an urgent need to pee. No wonder I'd conjured a bathroom in my dream!

But what about the man? He was so real. The security and acceptance I felt in his presence was beyond words, literally—our communication was all telepathic.

Who was he? Was he the spirit guide the psychics had mentioned?

I got my answer the following day. Dan and I were playing with the boys in the living room, and Geoffrey commandeered my attention. He grabbed two Fisher Price "Little People" from the table. Then he handed me the blond girl known as Sarah Lynn and kept the nameless, redheaded boy himself.

He moved the boy in tiny bounces that suggested footsteps along the table, then stopped in front of the girl in my hand. "Hi," he said, acting out a greeting. "How are you?"

"I'm fine," I replied, taking the girl's role. "How are you?"

"I'm fine too," Geoffrey said.

"I'm Sarah Lynn," I said, making the girl bow. "What's your name?"

Because the boy looked somewhat Irish, I thought Patrick would be a good name for him. But I wondered which name Geoffrey would choose.

He didn't bat an eye. "Michel," he said.

I did a double take. Then I realized the significance of the figures he'd chosen. I had the girl whose blond hair matched mine, and he had the boy with orange hair, which was about as close as Fisher Price came to auburn. And get this: Geoffrey now held "Michel" above the table so he hovered in the air in front of the girl.

I glanced around the room, as though I might spot the soul who'd inspired Geoffrey with the name. I didn't have to see him; I knew in my heart it was my spirit guide. Perhaps it was him I spotted on the stairs during the show on psychic children. Maybe he encouraged me to contact the adult twins so they could give me his name, which got the ball of communication rolling. Then, through the dream and through my son, he connected with me in a way I could understand.

As I said before, I'm not a professional psychic. If my guides are this close to me, yours are just as close. Are you ready to learn more about them? Here are some suggestions to get you started.

Clues from Childhood

These are important, particularly with your main guide. You also might've foreseen other guides who played, or will later play, a role.

Did you have an imaginary friend as a child? What was his/her name?

What names did you give your favorite dolls or stuffed animals?

Did you write stories as a child? Did one character in particular stand out or appear in several stories? Were details about that character clearer than other details? When you wrote dialogue, did that character's voice flow to you more easily than that of other characters?

If your memory is a little foggy or you want confirmation, you can ask childhood friends and neighbors, siblings, cousins, parents, grandparents, or other family members. The first indications of our guides often appear during childhood.

Dreams and Astral Trips

As we've seen, spirit guides enter our dreams on occasion. They also accompany us on many of our astral trips.

Astral projection—also known as an out-of-body experience (OBE)—is the natural ability of the astral body (spirit) to leave the physical body. While some disregard OBEs as mere fantasy or dreams, most of the people who have them swear that the experience is quite different. In *Have an Out-of-Body Experience in 30 Days: the Free Flight Program*, psychologist Keith Harary states that lab measurements of brain waves and other physiological functions taken while the phenomenon occurs support the reality of OBEs.

Astral travel is essentially the same as astral projection, except that we sometimes experience the journey as well as the destination. It's how we arrived in our bodies before birth and how we'll go Home again at death. And during brief but beneficial holidays from our bodies—two to three times a week, on average, while we sleep, according to Sylvia Browne—it's luggage-free transportation from our weighty, corporeal frames to the bliss of spiritual freedom. In *Conversations with God* (Book 3), "God" confirms that "in birth, the soul finds itself constricted within the awful limitations of a body, and at death escapes those constrictions again. It does the same thing again during sleep. Back to freedom the soul flies—and rejoices once again with the expression and experience of its true nature."

How can we tell when a "dream" is actually an astral outing? There are three dead giveaways: 1. a clear, rational sequence of events; 2. observing yourself from the outside, i.e., moving into and/or out of your body; and 3. flying or floating under your own power, without the aid of an airplane or other technology.

Of course, many astral journeys don't include the sensation of flight. It all depends on our speed of travel: a slow pace similar to a stroll; an intermediate speed during which a great, roaring wind seems to rush past us; or the speed of thought, which brings us instantaneously to our destination. The spirit can access all three of these speeds, and many of you will recognize them from your own experience. If the subject interests you, I suggest reading *Mastering Astral Projection: 90-day Guide to Out-of-Body Experience* by Robert Bruce and Brian Mercer.

If a dream—or an astral trip disguised as a dream—contains any of the following elements, it's a strong indication you've connected with one of your guides.

The shared, direct gaze

In my experience, guides don't blink once their gaze locks onto mine. Their eyes seem to bore into my soul, and I get the feeling they know me better than I do myself. The event inspires trust, not fear.

The disembodied voice

If you've watched any of the popular TV shows that feature paranormal investigations—e.g., *Ghost Hunters, Ghost Hunters International, Destination Truth, Paranormal State, Ghost Adventures,* etc.—you're already familiar with this common shout-out from the spirit world. If you're not, don't let it creep you out. Some people audibly hear their spirit guide's voice when they're wide awake. However, spirit guides know that most people will more easily hear and acknowledge their guide's voice during dreams, or what we believe are dreams. After all, that's when many of our preconceived notions and hang-ups fly out the window, so to speak. Angels, guardians, and guides can crank up the volume without our being too unnerved by the event and give us valuable information. So if you're in a dream and a voice without an obvious owner speaks to you, relax. There's a good chance it's your spirit guide.

Lucidity, specifics, and display of heretofore unknown abilities

When you find yourself analyzing the events of your dream even as you participate in them, you're having a lucid dream. With that awareness, you'll notice a number of specific details, many of which you can commit to memory. You might also notice that you can speak a language you never learned in your present life or use skills you don't remember acquiring. In many cases, someone you perceive as a friend and/or mentor will be at your side and will probably be your guide.

The act of following someone you intuitively sense is trustworthy

There's often a sense of expectation when this occurs, as if something important waits just around the corner. You may not know why; you simply feel drawn to the individual and follow without question. If for some reason you're reluctant to trust other people, your guides might first appear to you as appealing animals, not only in dreams but in meditation, too. It's in their best interest and yours to help you feel comfortable.

Even when they assume a human form, their initial appearance or clothing could disturb you, depending on your personal preferences, past experiences, or current situation. If such a thing happens, they'll withdraw for a bit, and the next time they appear, they'll do it in a way that's more acceptable to you. Just bear in mind their intention is not to deceive you, but to befriend you.

Visitations

As you already know, spirits pop in to say hello on occasion. Our guides are around—frequently right beside us—a good deal of the time, but we don't always detect them.

As you warm up to them, however, there will be times when you experience a sudden, undeniable sense of *knowing* not just that they're present, but their precise location in a room. And if they think you can handle physical contact without jumping out of your skin, they might announce their presence through a gentle tingle which feels lighter than a human's touch on your forehead, your shoulders, an arm, or elsewhere.

Psychic Hits

These can come from you, your family, a friend, professional psychics, or even strangers on the street. Don't write them off as fantasy...especially when they corroborate each other. Pay attention!

When confirmation and synchronicity occur, don't write them off as mere coincidence. Open yourself up to the built-in guidance and magic of our interconnected universe.

Historical Research

Although several ascended masters may work with you during this life, their guidance won't be limited to you alone. They oversee the spiritual development of many people and are available to anyone who asks for their assistance. Additionally, your personal guides are more likely to be total unknowns than famous historic figures. Still, you might get lucky and discover that your guides—and details about them—match up with individuals recorded somewhere in history, even if just on Ancestry.com. Depending on the information they and your psychic senses give you, you may start with scant clues or an arsenal of facts. Either way, if you do the research, you could learn a lot more about them and—if you knew them in previous lives—about yourself.

Channeling and Meditation

As with most things in life, patience and persistence pay off when dealing with channeling and meditation. Answers will come to you. They might pop into your mind as clairvoyant images, which are visual symbols for thought, or in the form of words, which are really just verbal and written symbols for thought. When it comes to symbology, words are usually more straightforward than visions, but don't stress over it. Whatever form of information you receive is a gift, and quite frankly, a given. The spirits you want to contact *want you to contact them.* Just your intention to communicate will set in motion a chain of events that will ultimately help you succeed.

The channeling technique I described in chapter 5 also works with spirit guides. Just make sure you ask specifically for their input.

If meditation appeals to you, you can create your own meditation or try a guided one on CD. There's a wealth of such CDs out there. You could look online or in a local bookstore and let your angels, guardians, and/or guides lead you to the best version for you. On the Internet, a specific title might stand out to you and continually draw your attention even as you're checking other titles. In a store, a specific CD might happen to fall off the shelf or be placed apart from the others in an odd and noticeable place. In most cases, your intuition—or the spirits who use it to communicate with you—will inform your choice.

You can also meet your spirit guide through the following meditation. After the initial three steps (stating your intention, grounding and cleansing, and focused relaxation), your starting point will be the comfortable room you created for the Guardian Angel meditation.

Meditation for Meeting Spirit Guides

Imagine yourself walking about your ideal room, doing anything you want to do inside it. Soon you decide to take a stroll in the garden outside. You exit the room and head down a hall toward a table beside the back door. On the table is a round, willow basket with a braided handle. You grab the basket by its handle and head out the door into the fresh air. Breathing in the scent of flowers, you walk through a lush garden toward a cedar hedge maze at the far end. The hedge is seven feet high, and the maze forms the shape of a spiral.

You enter the maze and, after a few steps, you spy a red gemstone the size of a golf ball on the ground. Crouching to get a closer look, you realize it's a ruby. You pluck it from the ground and stand. Then you study the ruby in your hand. The color fills you with strength and courage, and it seems to enhance your sensory awareness. After a minute, you drop the ruby into your basket and continue forward.

After a bit, you notice a second object on the ground: an orange-gold chunk of amber. You stoop to pick it up, then straighten. Its edges are smooth, and you feel balanced and positive as you stare into its depths. Moments later, you place it in the basket and move on.

You round another curve of the tall maze and discover a shiny, yellow crystal—the same size as your other treasures—called citrine. You collect it, too, and are suddenly struck with a sense of mental and emotional clarity. The crystal energizes you and rouses your confidence. Smiling, you put it in the basket and continue walking.

Deeper into the spiral, you see an emerald on the ground. You pick it up, and almost immediately, a sense of peace pervades you. Your heart swells with love, and you feel completely safe and secure. You drop the emerald into the basket and go further into the maze.

The next gemstone you spot is a blue sapphire. This you've got to have, so you lift it from the ground and squeeze it gently in the palm of your hand. The deep color inspires you, and although you're not sure why, you get the impression that just by holding it, the sapphire heightens your ability to hear messages from Spirit. Into the basket it goes, and you amble onward.

Soon, you glimpse an amethyst. As your hand closes around this purple gem, your psychic awareness increases, and you surrender to its power. You are willing and able to see whatever your guide(s) will show you. The amethyst goes into the basket, and you continue forward.

Up ahead is a clear quartz cluster the size of your palm. You pick it up and detect a slight vibration within it. Mesmerized, you study the crystal's unique shape and allow its gentle hum to harmonize you with your surroundings. It taps into that part of you that is one with everything in existence, and you know in your bones that you are now ready to meet your guide.

You round the final bend and there, at the heart of the spiral, is your main guide. Is it a man or a woman? Note his/her clothing. Ask his/her name. Is your guide doing something or simply looking at you? If you glimpse a symbol instead of an actual being, memorize its details as best you can. If you're only aware of a specific scent, try to identify it.

Offer your basket to the guide and note his/her response. Remember, your spirit guide knows and loves you just as you are, but his/her appearance may shift and change as the meeting continues. Spend as much time with your guide as you like. If other guides appear, discover what you can about them, too.

When you're ready, say goodbye. You can either retrieve your basket of goodies or leave it with your guide(s). Follow the maze in reverse until you step back out into the open garden.

(End of meditation)

Take a few deep breaths and open your eyes. Reflect on your experience, and if you want to keep a record, write down everything you remember about the guide(s) you encountered and what you learned.

10

Animal Guides:
Helpers, Totems,
and Omens

By now, you're well aware that human spirits aren't the only guides around. Whether incarnate, in spirit, or symbolic—e.g., associated with specific archangels—animals also do the job. They facilitate our spiritual growth and remind us of our potential. They can teach, warn, and comfort us and clarify even the most confusing situations.

Animal spirits and human spirits have many similarities, two of which deserve mention here. A guide can function as a guardian, just as a guardian can play the role of a guide. This is also true of other guardians such as ascended masters or nature spirits. It's also worth noting that though one or more are strongest in your life, others come and go as needed.

In chapter 8, I mentioned power/totem animals. Believers in these animal helpers hold a variety of views on the subject; sifting through the information can make your head spin! Even though totems—like everything else—originate in the spirit world, some see them only as ancestral guardians, quite separate from "spirit animals" who serve as messengers. Others distinguish between "power totem animals" (part of shamanic faiths) and "spirit totem animals," although both can stay with you for life. Still others, like D. J. Conway and Silver Raven-Wolf, believe power animals and "familiars" are one and the same.

Many are adamant that a *true* shaman or witch must be chosen and accepted by a power totem, which might be a familiar or a "fetch" (a spirit or deity who sends forth an animal spirit, or actually takes the form of an animal spirit, when first approaching a potential student). However, since we choose our key experiences—together with allies and enemies alike—on the Other Side before we're ever born, a different picture emerges. In an environment of cooperation and mutual respect for all parties concerned, humans and animals choose *each other*.

It's not my intention to get anyone's knickers in a twist over terminology or power comparisons. Nor would I wish to commercialize the beliefs of *any* culture, ancient or otherwise. Just know that when I use the word "totem," I do so with the utmost respect for totemistic societies and all animal spirits, be they attached to a physical body or not.

A Word About Familiars

Familiars are a type of "helper guide" and guardian, and they can be physical or astral (spirit) animals, human spirits, elementals, and even plants. In *Animal Magick: the Art of Recognizing and Working with Familiars*, D. J. Conway describes familiars of the animal kind and asserts that you don't have to be a witch or even believe in familiars to have one. Pets sometimes function as familiars and communicate by sending you mental pictures.

"You may even have an astral-bodied animal familiar, drawn to you by your enthusiasm for that particular creature with which it is impossible to have contact in the physical realm," she explains. "Many people collect pictures or little statues of a particular creature and never consciously realize they are subconsciously communicating with that creature, either as a non-magick-working familiar or for the magickal and spiritual powers it has."

In this way, familiars are very like totem animals (which we'll discuss in a moment), life totems in particular. They embody all of the positive characteristics of their species.

Silver RavenWolf acknowledges this fact in *To Ride a Silver Broomstick: New Generation Witchcraft* and states that the term "power animal" denotes a witch's connection to the essence of that animal's power. Furthermore, "in the astral, you can merge with your totem and become the animal with your own intelligence intact. This is called shapeshifting."

Possible Identities/ Interpretations of Animal Spirits

When you encounter an animal spirit—in dreams, meditation, or "real" life—it could be one of three things: 1. the actual spirit of an animal; 2. an energetic representative for a whole species of animal, not an individual one; or 3. an entity, as in an angel or other spirit, using that animal image to communicate with the human world. (See the animals that correspond to specific archangels in chapter 3.)

As Ted Andrews points out in his book *Animal-Speak*, "We do not have to believe that these images and totems are beings of great intelligence, but there are archetypal powers that reside behind and oversee all manifestations in Nature. These archetypes have their own qualities and characteristics which are reflected in the behaviors and activities of animals and other expressions of Nature. When we pay attention to and acknowledge a nature totem, we are honoring the essence that lies behind it. We are opening up and attuning to that essence. We can then use it to understand our own life circumstances more clearly. We can share in its power or 'medicine.' Nature totems—especially animals—are symbols of specific kinds of energy we are manifesting and aligning with in our life."

Totem Animals

We are inextricably linked with the natural world. It doesn't just support us; it *is* us. And keep in mind, everything labeled "supernatural" is actually natural; we just don't comprehend it fully ... yet. On an energetic level, our environment is merely an extension of our own bodies.

An itch on the back of your hand, which is a natural extension of your body, is a message that draws your attention and causes you to scratch. When creatures—whether flesh-and-blood, spirit, or symbol—come to call, they also serve as our extended body and give us messages that can guide our actions. This is especially true when their appearance is unusual, unexpected, and/or recurring. They influence us through four major roles: the life totem (life animal), journey totem (journey animal), message totem (message animal), and shadow totem (shadow animal). Let's examine all four.

Life Totem

This animal is the one I introduced in chapter 8. It's your lifelong guardian and guide from the spirit realm. It reflects your deeper, spiritual self and your innate abilities—some of which you could be unaware of—and it just might offer clues to the destiny you planned before birth.

After all, you chose your totem before you were born, as Sylvia Browne explains in *Phenomenon*, and it's a faithful companion, devoted to your welfare. "We would never consider venturing to earth without our totem," she writes, "and along with every pet we've ever owned in every lifetime we've lived on earth, our totem is among the first to greet us when we complete our trip through the tunnel and arrive safely back Home."

When necessary, this animal calls upon other animal spirits to communicate specific information and encourage your growth. It oversees their guidance and can actually work with the other spirits; in this way, it can function as a guide.

Journey Totem

This animal arrives when a new life path opens up for you. The length of that path and your progress along it determine how long it remains. It will stay with you until you complete that particular journey.

Message Totem

Unless you're too stubborn to get the hint, this animal stays for a brief period of time and will leave a strong impression on you. It might suggest the best way to handle a current challenge. It might also function as an omen.

An omen is a prophetic sign, and it can occur on a personal level or on a large scale. In *Animal Omens*, Victoria Holt explains how personal omens can guide us. They teach us to observe the world around us and to use our intuition. They give us insight into life situations and events.

On a larger scale, animals can warn us of future catastrophes. Psychic and interspecies intuitive Frances

Fox believes that dolphins predicted the 2005 Hurricane Katrina disaster weeks before it happened. On January 4, 2005, in an article for National Geographic News, journalist Maryann Mott reported curious details concerning the 2004 Indian Ocean Tsunami: "Before giant waves slammed into Sri Lanka and India coastlines ten days ago, wild and domestic animals seemed to know what was about to happen and fled to safety. According to eyewitness accounts, the following events happened:

- Elephants screamed and ran for higher ground.
- Dogs refused to go outdoors.
- Flamingos abandoned their low-lying breeding areas.
- Zoo animals rushed into their shelters and could not be enticed to come back out."

Of course, belief in animal omens has been around since ancient times.

Shadow Totem

This animal is one you initially fear but later acknowledge as an ally. It will likely repulse you and show up again and again while you struggle to make peace with its presence. It may represent a hidden strength or a weakness you won't admit. Don't be surprised if it appears during times of great hardship or chaos. Once you've identified it, remember it's only there to help and to point the way toward a better version of yourself than you ever imagined.

Interpreting an animal's presence

Context is crucial when interpreting the meaning of an animal's appearance in your world. Each animal is associated with a number of qualities, and any one of them might fit the bill. The specific quality and attendant message will be unique to your situation. Animals can also coax information from our subconscious minds into our conscious awareness. Here's an example.

One night, I dreamed I was standing at my kitchen counter, sorting clusters of herbs. The cabinet at face level opened to reveal a raccoon. It jumped onto the counter, looked me in the eye, and scratched my hand. Abruptly, I awoke, certain the dream was important. I soon learned that the word "raccoon" was thought to derive from the Algonquian Indian word *arckunem,* which meant "hand-scratcher." Raccoons can be symbols of curiosity, protection, dexterity, or disguise, but in this instance, the dream wasn't an omen. Rather, the raccoon saw through my present "disguise" and reminded me of a past life in which I spoke Meskwaki-Sauk (an Algonquian language) and used herbal medicine to help others.

The symbols and signs that communicate meaning and guidance can appear anywhere. Let's say you dream about a statue that has a human body but an elephant head, and you have no idea what it represents. The next day, your children have a lengthy chat about elephants for no apparent reason and try to imitate them. Then, later that same day, the very same creature appears as the first image on the screen when you flick on the television. To top it all off, you and your spouse end the day by watching a favorite TV show, a fast-paced, fictional series that should have nothing whatsoever to do with elephants. A featured character that night just happens to be Ganesh, a Hindu god who shapeshifts into an elephant during the episode.

What would you think then? Would you chalk it up to coincidence? Or would you start to suspect someone or some*thing* working behind the scenes to give you a message?

With a little research, you'd discover that Ganesh— who is usually depicted with a human body and the head of an elephant—is known as the remover of obstacles. If your efforts to accomplish a goal have been blocked at every turn, the recurring elephant symbol could signal relief and ultimate success.

When an animal shows up in your experience— either repeatedly or once in an unusual or obvious way— check the symbolism associated with it. Then apply your personal situation (the context) and your own intuition, and you'll get the message. If you're still unsure, ask your guardians and/or guides for clarification.

You can also open yourself to an animal's energy, or message, by focusing on its image in one of two ways: 1. using an actual photo, drawing, or sculpture of the animal; 2. conjuring a picture of the animal in your mind. Before beginning either exercise, make sure you're alone and won't be disturbed, then take a deep, calming breath.

For the first method, stare at the animal's likeness and ask any questions you might have. You can also forego questions and simply empty your mind to receive whatever comes. If you favor clairsentience, touch the picture or hold the sculpture to help you tune in.

For the second method, close your eyes and see the animal in your mind's eye. Concentrate on the image, and when you feel ready, ask questions or simply remain quiet and receptive.

Below is a list of the most common totem animals and meanings associated with them, collected from several sources, including the works of Ted Andrews, D. J. Conway, Victoria Hunt, Jamie Sams, and David Carson. For a more comprehensive list and greater detail, check out Andrews's *Animal-Speak* and Conway's *Animal Magick*, or another related book in the recommended reading list.

Alligator and Crocodile—initiation, integration, primal energies of birth and motherhood

Ant—diligence, discipline, order, patience

Antelope—action, flexibility of the mind, speed

Armadillo—boundaries, empathy, personal protection

Badger—assertiveness, bold self-expression, determination

Bat—initiation, rebirth, transition

Bear—awakening the power of the unconscious, balance, introspection

Beaver—building dreams, setting goals

Bee—cooperation with others, extracting the "honey" from life, fertility

Beetle—regeneration, resurrection

Bison (Buffalo)—abundance, manifestation

Blackbird—energy, new awareness and understanding of the forces of nature

Bluebird—modesty, quiet confidence and joy

Blue Jay—development of creative talents, proper use of power

Boar—direction, protection, warrior spirit

Bobcat—new learning, secrets, silence

Bull—fertility, stability

Butterfly—joy, movement, transformation

Camel—fortitude, patience, use of resources

Canary—power of song and voice

Cardinal—renewed vitality, self-worth

Caribou—adaptability, mobility, physical fitness, travel

Cat—independence, magic, mystery, self-assurance

Centipede—coordination, synchronization

Chameleon—auric sensitivity, clairvoyance, mastering change

Cheetah—decisive action, precision

Chickadee—cheerful and truthful expression

Chipmunk—balance between caution and trust, curiosity, respect

Cougar—coming into your own power, courage, leadership

Cow—contentment, gentleness, motherhood, nourishment, plenty

Coyote—balance between wisdom and folly, duality, humor, insight, playfulness

Crane—creation through focus, longevity

Cricket—good luck, self-expression, song

Crow—divine law, magic of creation, shapeshifting

Cuckoo—flowing with the tide (not against it), herald of new fate, living in "the now"

Deer—gentleness, innocence, spiritual knowledge, swiftness, unconditional love

Dinosaur—ancient wisdom, primitive power

Dog—companionship, loyalty, protection

Dolphin (Porpoise)—ancient wisdom, harmony, intelligence, joy, life energy, power of breath

Dove—kindness, love, peace, prophecy

Dragon—conscious awareness, power and magic of the land, protection

Dragonfly and Damselfly—adaptability, illusion, mystical messages, power of light

Duck—bonding, emotional security, free will

Eagle—enlightenment, spiritual connection to higher realms, strength of spirit, vision

Elephant—ancient power, loyalty, patience, remover of obstacles, strength

Elk—freedom, stamina, nobility, strength

Emu—feeling grounded, practicality, reason

Falcon—agility, astral travel, questioning, vision, watchfulness

Ferret—cleverness, playfulness, resourcefulness, solving mysteries, stealth

Finch—activity, desire, new experiences, variety

Firefly—communication, illumination, sharing of self

Flamingo—higher perspective, maturity, open-heartedness

Fox—camouflage, cunning, discretion, invisibility, shapeshifting

Frog—cleansing, emotional healing, transformation through water and sound

Giraffe—farsightedness, functioning above and beyond the accepted norm, new horizons

Goat—new endeavors, persistence, progress

Goldfinch—awakening to nature spirits, positive attitude

Goose—the call of the quest, inspiration, providence, safe return, travel to places of legend

Grackle—overcoming excess and blocked emotions, seeing beyond the obvious

Grasshopper—trusting your inner voice, uncanny leaps forward

Groundhog (Woodchuck)—altered states of consciousness, decisions, solitude

Grouse—sacred dancing and drumming

Gull (Herring/Sea)—persistence, responsible behavior and communication, versatility

Hawk—awareness, guardianship, messages, observation, truth, visionary power

Hedgehog—boundaries, self-preservation

Hen—creativity, feminine power, fertility, nurturing

Heron—self-determination, self-reliance, vigilance

Horse—exploration, freedom, power, travel

Hummingbird—celebration, joy, optimism, wonder

Hyena—laughter, speed in achieving a goal

Jackal—alertness, cleverness, solitude

Jaguar—forest spirits, healing, hidden knowledge, integrity, messages, psychic empowerment

Jellyfish—flexibility, intent, maintaining balance

Kangaroo—guardianship, moving forward in leaps

Kestrel—proper values

Koala—clairaudience, feeling comfortable with being alone, thoughtfulness

Ladybug—delight, surprises, trust, unexpected gifts

Lark—freedom from worry

Leopard—boldness, confidence, power of choice, stealth

Lion—courage, pride, strength, trusting feminine energies

Lizard—dreaming, letting go, subtlety of perception

Llama—ability to carry a burden, comforting others, expression of opinions and preferences

Loon—imagination, lucid dreaming, revival of old hopes and wishes, serenity

Lynx—ability to truly listen, instinct, mystical secrets, silence, solitude

Magpie—boldness, familiars, occult knowledge, proper use of intelligence

Manatee—contentment, gentleness, innocence, love

Meadowlark—cheerful reflection, enjoyment of the journey, playfulness

Mockingbird—counseling, discovery of one's purpose, recognition of innate abilities

Mole—improvisation, retrieval, stealth

Mongoose—cleverness, courage, playfulness, resourcefulness

Monkey—benevolence, community, curiosity, ingenuity, parenthood

Moose—assertiveness, self-esteem, spontaneity

Moth—clear perception, movement from shadow into the light, out-of-body exploration

Mountain Lion—decisiveness, leadership, personal power, strength

Mountain Goat—seeking new heights, surefootedness

Mouse—attention to detail, organization, scrutiny

Mule—acceptance, humility

Newt—miracles, power of observation

Nuthatch—grounding of faith, higher wisdom

Octopus—intelligence, protection through distraction, versatility

Opossum—sensibility, strategy, the use of appearances

Oriole—positive change, positive relationship with nature, weaving light into any situation

Ostrich—becoming grounded, good judgment

Otter—curiosity, joy, playfulness, sharing

Owl—astral projection, clairvoyance, insight, magic, vision, wisdom

Ox—chastity, reliability, sacredness, sacrifice

Panther—embracing the unknown, reclaiming one's true power

Parakeet—curiosity, hospitality, lighthearted conversation

Parrot—communication, diplomacy, power of light and colors

Peacock—dignity, heightened vision, immortality, pride, self-confidence, visualization, wisdom

Pegasus—beauty, immortality, magic, power, supernatural strength

Pelican—hidden resources, rising above life's trials, selflessness

Penguin—astral projection, family orientation, lucid dreaming, unity

Pheasant—concealment, family fertility, sexuality

Phoenix—renewal, transformation

Pig—ancestral knowledge, intellect, strong emotions

Pigeon—return to the love and security of home

Porcupine—humility, innocence, renewal of wonder, trust

Prairie Dog—community, preparedness, productivity, swiftness

Praying Mantis—contemplation, positive focus, power of stillness

Quail—group harmony, sanctuary, teamwork, tolerance

Rabbit (Hare)—alertness, conquering fear, fertility, hidden skills, new life

Raccoon—curiosity, dexterity, disguise, protection

Ram—achievement, breakthroughs, determination, seeking new beginnings, strength, virility

Rat—resourcefulness, shrewdness, stealth, success

Raven—creation, exploration of the unknown, introspection, magic, shapeshifting

Rhinoceros—ancient wisdom, determination, follow-through, forcefulness

Roadrunner—mental and physical agility and speed

Robin—freshness, parenthood, reliability, spread of new growth

Rooster (Cock)—ambition, resurrection, sexuality, vigilance

Salamander—camouflage, clear perception, power/medicine of fire, quick response

Salmon—inspiration, instinct, persistence, rejuvenation, wisdom

Scorpion—self-defense, stinging truth

Sea Lion and Seal—cleverness, curiosity, imagination, intuition, lucid dreaming

Seahorse—androgyny, confidence, fatherhood, grace, uniqueness

Shark—adaptability, signs, survival, warning

Sheep—congeniality, group comfort, patience, warmth

Shrimp—recognition, scavenging

Skunk—presence, reputation, respect

Snail—determination, perseverance, self-protection

Snake—death and rebirth, life force, sexual potency, transmutation

Snow Leopard—overcoming one's demons, renewal of vision and vitality

Sparrow—awakening of dignity and self-worth, triumph of common nobility

Spider—creativity, the weaving of fate, writing

Squirrel—activity, gathering, preparation, thrift, trust

Starling—etiquette, group dynamics

Starfish—expansion, hope, inspiration

Stork—birth (and rebirth), growth, unspoken communication

Swallow—proper perspective, protection and warmth for the home

Swan—awakening one's true beauty and power, grace, surrender

Swift—agility and speed in the "Great Quest" (spiritual alchemy), overcoming hesitation

Tiger—devotion, passion, power, sensuality, unexpected lessons, valor

Turkey—generosity, harvest, sacrifice, shared blessings

Turtle—Earth Mother, fertility, healing, motherhood, nurturing, protection, waking the senses (all of them, including the psychic ones)

Unicorn—connection to woodland beings, magic, love, purity, wishes fulfilled

Vulture—death and rebirth, new vision, purification, release

Weasel—clairaudience, ingenuity, silent observation or pursuit, stealth

Whale—gentleness, intuition, power of song, record keeping, telepathy

Wolf—guardianship, knowledge, loyalty, pathfinder, ritual, Spirit, teacher

Wolverine—fearlessness, tenacity

Woodpecker—devotion, good judgment, the power of rhythm, protection, sensitivity

Wren—boldness, desire to do great things, resourcefulness, Spirit

Yak—ancient wisdom, healing stiffness or numbness, understanding higher purpose

Zebra—balance, individuality, nonjudgment

A to Z, those are some of the animals you might encounter—in the flesh, in spirit, or through imagery—during this visit to earth. If a meaning doesn't resonate with you, trust your instinct. The animal will likely feed you the correct message through a gut feeling, a mental picture, or a vocal cue. Not unlike the fictional Dr. Dolittle, we can talk to the animals. In their own way, they can speak to us, too.

If you simply want to learn your main/life totem's identity and interact with it, use the Meditation for Meeting Spirit Guides from the previous chapter. When you encounter your totem in the center of the maze, pay close attention to its movements and anything it shows you. When it gazes into your eyes, what do you hear, smell, or sense otherwise? You just might encounter your spirit guide and totem at the same time; they're well aware of each other in the spirit world. Whatever occurs, review and/or write down your impressions after the meditation.

CONCLUSION

Angels, guardians, and guides are real. My experience and communications with them have enhanced my life in infinite ways. I wish the same for you.

To that end, I asked the angels if there was a message I should give you in this conclusion. Here's what they said:

NOTHING AND NO ONE CAN TRULY HARM YOU. WE ARE EVER BY YOUR SIDE. WE ARE YOUR FRIENDS, YOUR HELPERS, YOUR LOVING SUPPORT FOR ALL TIME. NO ONE COULD DISSUADE US FROM OUR TASK, NOT EVEN YOU. YOU CANNOT HIDE ANYTHING FROM US, NOR SHOULD YOU WANT TO. YOU ARE LOVED, PERIOD. TRUST. BELIEVE. SHINE.

It puts me in mind of William Shakespeare's Sonnet 116, which describes true love as "an ever-fixed mark that looks on tempests and is never shaken."

That's the kind of love our angels, guardians, and guides have for us. Get to know them, and you'll be awed and humbled by what you experience. They will quite literally add a new dimension to your life and help you grow into the person you've always wanted to be.

By tuning in to their love and wisdom, you won't just *hope* you have spiritual support; you'll *know* it. Your awareness and trust will blossom, and you'll know for certain that love and wisdom also reside in you.

$\mathcal{A}$PPENDIX:

———

*Specific Needs and Angels
and Ascended Masters Who Can Help*

Abundance: Archangel Zadkiel

Addictions, overcoming: Archangel Cassiel, Archangel Raphael, Babaji, Serapis Bey

Airline safety: Saint Thérèse

Alchemy: Archangel Raziel, Archangel Uriel, Saint-Germain

Animals: Archangel Ariel, Archangel Chamuel, Archangel Raphael, Saint Francis

Answered prayers: Archangel Sandalphon, Jesus, Mother Mary

Arguments, resolving: Archangel Raguel, Archangel Uriel, Archangel Zadkiel, Jesus, Serapis Bey

Artistic projects: Archangel Gabriel, Archangel Jophiel, Serapis Bey

Authority figures, dealing with: Moses, Saint-Germain

Balance: Buddha, Melchizedek, Yogananda

Beauty: Archangel Jophiel

Breathwork: Babaji

Career: Archangel Chamuel, Saint Francis

Chakra clearing: Archangel Michael, Melchizedek

Children: Archangel Gabriel, Archangel Metatron, Jesus, Mother Mary, Saint Francis, Saint Thérèse

Clairvoyance, increasing: Archangel Haniel, Archangel Ramiel, Archangel Raphael, Archangel Raziel

Clear communication with God: Archangel Sandalphon, Babaji, Jesus, Moses, Yogananda

Clearing negativity: Archangel Michael, Archangel Raphael, Archangel Zadkiel, Melchizedek, Saint-Germain, Solomon

Compassion: Archangel Zadkiel, Mother Mary

Confidence and poise: Archangel Haniel

Conviction (of beliefs): Archangel Michael

Color therapy: Melchizedek

Cooperation from others: Archangel Raguel

Courage: Archangel Michael, Moses, Saint-Germain

Crystals, knowledge and use of: Melchizedek

Decisiveness: El Morya

Detoxification: Archangel Raphael, Melchizedek

Defending the innocent: Archangel Raguel

Direction: Archangel Michael, Jesus, Saint-Germain

Divine magic: Archangel Ariel, Archangel Raziel, Solomon

Dreams, psychic: Archangel Ramiel

Earth changes: Archangel Uriel, Archangel Ariel, Archangel Chamuel, Melchizedek

Ego, rising above: Archangel Zadkiel, Buddha, Jesus, Moses

Empowerment: Archangel Raguel

Energy/vitality: Archangel Michael

Environmental concerns: Archangel Ariel, Archangel Chamuel, Saint Francis

Esoteric knowledge: Archangel Raziel, Melchizedek, Saint-Germain, Solomon

Exercise/physical fitness: Serapis Bey

Faith, strengthening: Archangel Raphael, El Morya, Jesus, Moses

Family harmony: Archangel Raguel, Serapis Bey

Feng Shui: Melchizedek

Focus: Kuthumi, Saint-Germain

Forgiveness: Archangel Zadkiel, Jesus, Saint Padre Pio

Gardening: Saint Thérèse

Goals, achieving: Archangel Cassiel, Archangel Chamuel, Saint-Germain

Grace: Archangel Haniel, Mother Mary

Grief, comfort during: Archangel Azrael, Archangel Cassiel

Groundedness: El Morya

Harmony (in general): Archangel Raguel, Archangel Uriel, Serapis Bey

Healers, guidance for: Archangel Haniel, Archangel Raphael, Jesus, Melchizedek, Saint Padre Pio

Healing: Archangel Ariel, Archangel Haniel, Archangel Raphael, Archangel Zadkiel, Babaji, Jesus, Melchizedek, Mother Mary, Saint Francis, Saint Padre Pio, Saint Thérèse, Yogananda

Journalism: Archangel Gabriel

Joy: Archangel Michael, Archangel Sandalphon, Buddha

Justice: Archangel Michael, Archangel Raguel

Kabbalah study: Archangel Uriel, Solomon

Leadership: Melchizedek, Moses

Legal matters: Archangel Raguel, El Morya

Life changes, making: Archangel Ramiel

Life purpose, finding/remembering and dedication to: Archangel Chamuel, Archangel Michael, Kuthumi, Saint Francis, Saint-Germain

Lost items, finding: Archangel Chamuel, Archangel Zadkiel

Love, opening up to: Archangel Chamuel, Archangel Sandalphon, Mother Mary

Manifestation (of desires): Archangel Ariel, Archangel Raziel, Babaji, Jesus, Melchizedek, Saint-Germain, Solomon

Mathematics: Archangel Metatron, Kuthumi, Melchizedek

Mechanical problems, fixing: Archangel Michael

Meditation: Babaji, Buddha, Jesus, Saint Padre Pio, Yogananda

Memory, improving: Archangel Zadkiel, Kuthumi

Mercy: Archangel Ramiel, Archangel Zadkiel, Mother Mary

Miracles: Babaji, Jesus, Moses, Mother Mary

Moon energy: Archangel Haniel

Motivation: Archangel Michael, Kuthumi, Serapis Bey

Music: Archangel Gabriel, Archangel Jophiel, Archangel Sandalphon

Organization/Order: Archangel Metatron, Archangel Raguel, Kuthumi

Patience: Archangel Cassiel, Babaji

Peace: Archangel Chamuel, Babaji, Buddha, Jesus, Kuthumi, Melchizedek, Saint Francis, Serapis Bey, Yogananda

Perseverance: Archangel Chamuel, Saint-Germain

Procrastination, conquering: Archangel Michael

Prophecy: Archangel Ramiel, Serapis Bey

Protection (from negativity or psychic attack): Archangel Michael, El Morya, Melchizedek, Saint-Germain

Protection (of animals): Archangel Ariel

Protection (of travelers): Archangel Raphael

Psychic ability, expanding: Archangel Haniel, Archangel Raziel

Recordkeeping: Archangel Metatron, Archangel Ramiel

Relationships, strengthening: Archangel Chamuel, Serapis Bey

Research/study: Archangel Uriel, Archangel Zadkiel, Serapis Bey

Self-esteem: Archangel Michael

Teaching: Archangel Metatron, Archangel Michael, Mother Mary

Wisdom: Solomon

Writing: Archangel Gabriel, Archangel Metatron, Archangel Uriel

Yoga: Babaji, Yogananda

RECOMMENDED READING

Andrews, Ted. *Animal-Speak: The Spiritual and Magical Powers of Creatures Great and Small*. St. Paul, MN: Llewellyn, 2001.

———. *How to Meet and Work with Spirit Guides*. Woodbury, MN: Llewellyn, 2005.

Bercholz, Samuel, ed. and Sherab Chödzin Kohn. *The Buddha and His Teachings*. Boston: Shambhala, 2002.

Brennan, Barbara Ann. *Hands of Light: a Guide to Healing Through the Human Energy Field*. New York: Bantam, 1988.

Browne, Sylvia. *Angels, Guides, and Ghosts* (audiobook, CD). Carlsbad, CA: Hay House, 2004.

———. *Life on the Other Side: a Psychic's Tour of the Afterlife* (audiobook, CD). Minneapolis, MN: HighBridge, 2005.

———. *Phenomenon: Everything You Need to Know About the Paranormal*. New York: Dutton, 2005.

———. *Psychic Children: Revealing the Intuitive Gifts and Hidden Abilities of Boys and Girls* (audiobook, CD). Minneapolis, MN: HighBridge, 2007.

Bruce, Robert, and Brian Mercer. *Mastering Astral Projection: 90-day Guide to Out-of-Body Experience*. Woodbury, MN: Llewellyn, 2004.

Buckland, Raymond. *Scottish Witchcraft: the History and Magick of the Picts*. St. Paul, MN: Llewellyn, 1993.

Budge, E. A. Wallis. *The Book of the Dead: The Papyrus of Ani, Egyptian Text Transliteration and Translation*. New York: Dover, 1967.

Campanelli, Pauline. *Ancient Ways: Reclaiming Pagan Traditions*. St. Paul, MN: Llewellyn, 1992.

Campbell, Joseph. *The Hero with a Thousand Faces*. Novato, CA: New World Library, 2008.

Charles, R. H., trans. *The Book of Enoch the Prophet*. New York: Weiser Books, 2003.

Chopra, Deepak. *The Spontaneous Fulfillment of Desire: Harnessing the Infinite Power of Coincidence*. New York: Three Rivers Press, 2004.

Conway, D. J. *Animal Magick: the Art of Recognizing and Working with Familiars*. Woodbury, MN: Llewellyn, 2007.

———. *Celtic Magic*. St. Paul, MN: Llewellyn, 1993.

———. *Guides, Guardians, and Angels: Enhance Relationships with Your Spiritual Companions*. Woodbury, MN: Llewellyn, 2009.

Dyer, Wayne W. *Manifest Your Destiny: the Nine Spiritual Principles for Getting Everything You Want.* New York: Harper Collins, 1997.

Eason, Cassandra. *Angel Magic: a Hands-on Guide to Inviting Divine Help into Your Everyday Life.* Woodbury, MN: Llewellyn, 2010.

Edward, John. *Understanding Your Angels and Meeting Your Guides* (audiobook, CD). Carlsbad, CA: Hay House, 2003.

Forman, Joan. *Haunted Royal Homes.* London: Harrap, 1987.

Furlong, David. *Working with Earth Energies: How to Tap into the Healing Powers of the Natural World.* London, England: Piatkus Books, 2003.

Gray, John. *Near Eastern Mythology.* New York: Peter Bedrick, 1985.

Gundarsson, Kveldulf. *Teutonic Magic: the Magical and Spiritual Practices of the Germanic Peoples.* St. Paul, MN: Llewellyn, 1990.

———. *Teutonic Religion: Folk Beliefs and Practices of the Northern Tradition.* St. Paul, MN: Llewellyn, 1993.

Harary, Keith and Pamela Weintraub. *Have an Out-of-Body Experience in 30 Days: the Free Flight Program.* New York: St. Martin's Press, 1989.

Hunt, Victoria. *Animal Omens.* Woodbury, MN: Llewellyn, 2008.

Lysette, Chantel. *The Angel Code: Your Interactive Guide to Angelic Communication.* Woodbury, MN: Llewellyn, 2010.

———. *Azrael Loves Chocolate; Michael's a Jock: An Insider's Guide to What Your Angels Are Really Like.* Woodbury, MN: Llewellyn, 2008.

McClain, Florence Wagner. *Past Life Regression.* St. Paul, MN: Llewellyn, 1985.

McCoy, Edain. *Witta: an Irish Pagan Tradition.* St. Paul, MN: Llewellyn, 1993.

Murdock, D. M. *Christ in Egypt: the Horus-Jesus Connection.* Seattle, WA: Stellar House Publishing, 2009.

O'Neill, Kim. *Communicating with Your Angels* (audio CD). Houston, TX: Casablanca Productions.

O'Neill, Kim. *How to Talk with Your Angels.* New York: Avon, 1995.

Pagels, Elaine. *Beyond Belief: The Secret Gospel of Thomas.* New York: Vintage, 2004.

———. *The Origin of Satan: How Christians Demonized Jews, Pagans, and Heretics.* New York: Vintage, 1996.

RavenWolf, Silver. *To Ride a Silver Broomstick: New Generation Witchcraft.* St. Paul, MN: Llewellyn, 1993.

Robinson, James M., ed. *The Nag Hammadi Library.* New York: HarperOne, 1990.

Ross, Anne. *The Pagan Celts.* London: Batsford, 1986.

Sams, Jamie, and David Carson. *Medicine Cards: the Discovery of Power Through the Ways of Animals.* Santa Fe, NM: Bear and Company, 1988.

Sitchin, Zecharia. *The 12th Planet.* New York: Harper, 1999.

Thorsson, Edred. *Northern Magic: Mysteries of the Norse, Germans and English*. St. Paul, MN: Llewellyn, 1992.

Trepp, Leo. *A History of the Jewish Experience: Eternal Faith, Eternal People*. Springfield, NJ: Behrman House, 2000.

Van Praagh, James. *Ghosts Among Us: Uncovering the Truth About the Other Side* (audiobook, CD). Old Saybrook, CT: Tantor Media, 2008.

Virtue, Doreen. *Angel Numbers 101*. Carlsbad, CA: Hay House, 2008.

———. *Angel Therapy: Healing Messages for Every Area of Your Life*. Carlsbad, CA: Hay House, 1997.

———. *Archangels and Ascended Masters: a Guide to Working and Healing with Divinities and Deities*. Carlsbad, CA: Hay House, 2003.

———. *Connecting with Your Angels: See, Talk, and Work with the Angelic Realm* (audiobook, CD). Carlsbad, CA: Hay House Radio, 2004.

———. *Divine Guidance: How to Have a Dialogue with God and Your Guardian Angels* (audiobook, CD). New York: Audio Renaissance, 1998.

———. *Fairies 101: an Introduction to Connecting, Working, and Healing with the Fairies and Other Elementals*. Carlsbad, CA: Hay House, 2007.

Von Däniken, Erich. *Chariots of the Gods*. New York: Berkley Trade, 1999.

Walsch, Neale Donald. *Conversations with God: an Uncommon Dialogue (Book 1)*. Charlottesville, VA: Hampton Roads, 1995.

———. *Conversations with God: an Uncommon Dialogue (Book 2)*. Charlottesville, VA: Hampton Roads, 1997.

———. *Conversations with God: an Uncommon Dialogue (Book 3)*. Charlottesville, VA: Hampton Roads, 1998.

———. *Friendship with God: an Uncommon Dialogue*. New York: Putnam, 1999.

Webster, Richard. *Communicating with the Archangel Gabriel for Inspiration and Reconciliation*. St. Paul, MN: Llewellyn, 2005.

———. *Communicating with the Archangel Michael for Guidance and Protection*. St. Paul, MN: Llewellyn, 2004.

———. *Communicating with the Archangel Raphael for Healing and Creativity*. St. Paul, MN: Llewellyn, 2005.

———. *Encyclopedia of Angels*. Woodbury, MN: Llewellyn, 2009.

———. *Praying with Angels*. Woodbury, MN: Llewellyn, 2007.

Wiseman, Sara. *Your Psychic Child: How to Raise Intuitive and Spiritually Gifted Kids of All Ages*. Woodbury, MN: Llewellyn, 2010.

Yogananda, Paramahansa. *Autobiography of a Yogi*. Los Angeles: Self-Realization Fellowship, 2000.

ONLINE RESOURCES

Aaron Leitch—*kheph777.tripod.com*

The Bible and Anthroposophy—
www.bibleandanthroposophy.com

Catholic Online—*www.catholic.org*

Cosmic Harmony: The State of Enlightenment—
www.cosmicharmony.com

Crystalinks: Metaphysics and Science Website—
www.crystalinks.com

The Curious Dreamer—*www.thecuriousdreamer.com*

Encyclopedia Britannica—*www.britannica.com*

Geoffreyhodson.com: An esoteric resource on
the life and work of Geoffrey Hodson—
www.geoffreyhodson.com

Hidden Ireland: A guide to Irish fairies—
www.irelandseye.com

International World History Project—
www.history-world.org

Internet Sacred Text Archive—*www.sacred-texts.com*

Marypages—*www.marypages.com*

Miracles of the Saints—*www.miraclesofthesaints.com*

themystica.org: Home of the encyclopedias the *Mystica*
and *Mythical-Folk*—*www.themystica.org*

National Geographic News—*www.nationalgeographic.com*

New World Encyclopedia—*www.newworldencyclopedia.org*

Richard Ebbs Web Site—*www.feedback.nildram.co.uk*

Spirit Walk Ministry: A Shamanic Studies Ministry—
www.spiritwalkministry.com

Theosophy Library Online—*www.theosophy.org*